PROPHETIC TRANSFORMATION

Jonathan Allen

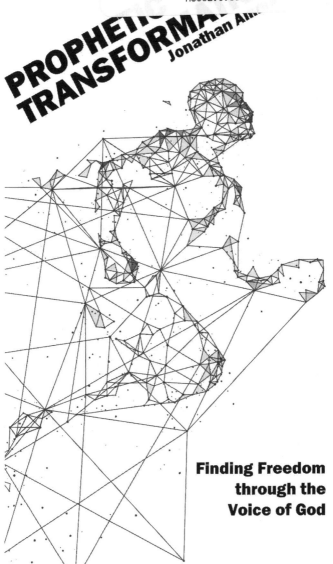

**Finding Freedom
through the
Voice of God**

SUPERNATURAL TRUTH PRODUCTIONS, LLC
Practical Training for Spirit-Filled Living
www.SupernaturalTruth.com

Copyright © 2018, Jonathan Ammon (Sentlives.com)

Underlining and bolding in scripture quotations reflect the author's added emphasis.

Please note that Supernatural Truth Productions, LLC, chooses to capitalize various pronouns and metaphors used for the Father, the Son, and the Holy Spirit, even when such capitalization does not exist in an original source, including Bible translations. This is a style decision made for the sake of honoring God in our text.

ISBN: 0-9988171-2-0
ISBN-13: 978-0-9988171-2-5

TABLE of CONTENTS

PART 4: THE WEAPONS OF OUR WARFARE

DEDICATION

For the bride.

ACKNOWLEDGEMENTS

I would like to thank the Father for adopting, correcting, and loving me; Jesus, for rescuing me and being the initiator and finisher of my faith; the Holy Spirit, for convicting me and pouring love into my heart.

Thank you Tatiana for your love, support, and grounded reminders that God's voice is clear and simple.

My parents deserve more thanks than I can give. Thank you for loving and serving me solely for the sake of relationship. This book is full of growing pains. You felt them too.

Thanks to Chuck Wood for loving me and encouraging me. It's often hard to think about your love and sacrifice for me without tears.

Thanks to Art Thomas for consistently representing the powerful Jesus who is a more than capable sanctifier. Thank you for letting me borrow your hope.

Thanks to Aaron Palmquist for being a big brother and friend. Thank you for your constant honesty and encouragement during this project. This book is far better because of you.

Thank you, Jim Gay. I am the man I am today because of your love and service when I was nasty piece of work. Thanks for not killing me and burying me beneath the campus chapel.

Thank you, Teresa Crumpton, for your unending faith in authors and writing. Your joy in the written word has infected me, and your work on this book and on my development as a writer has been invaluable.

I am immensely grateful to the numerous teachers and authors whose shoulders I stand on and from whom I have stolen liberally.

Hey, Jesus. We did it.

FOREWORD

by Art Thomas

There are few people in this world whose purposeful love and example have made a profound and lasting impact on my life and ministry. Jonathan Ammon is near the top of the list.

When Jonathan and I met, I was a young evangelist, just a short time into my new traveling ministry. He would come with me to speaking engagements, drive through the night with me, and dream out loud with me as we contemplated Jesus and His mission. With God's help, the little seeds in those conversations have grown to bear tremendous fruit as Jonathan and I continue in ministry throughout the world today.

As you read this book, I expect you to be equally challenged by Jonathan's transparency, depth, and passion for the Gospel. And I trust his emphasis on the presently-active voice of the Lord will awaken a fresh enthusiasm for the prophetic in your life, as it has mine.

When some people see the word "prophetic"—especially in the title of a book like this one—their minds might drift to weird excesses they may have witnessed throughout the last few decades of Christianity. Others may think of angry finger-pointing or hyperbolic rants about sin in our culture. But when my friend Jonathan uses that word, he's not talking about any of that nonsense. He's talking about genuine encounters with the presently-spoken words of the Lord—sometimes comforting, sometimes challenging, and always loving.

I know few people who so zealously contend for true expressions of the voice of God. Jonathan is not interested in obscure flights of the imagination that pacify us into thinking we have a vibrant faith (when really it's nothing more than self-aggrandizing fluff that bears no real fruit). He's not even all that interested in sweet little words of encouragement that could *possibly* be God but could just as easily come from the person's own mind (not that he's opposed to encouragement or the subtle "I love you's" of Jesus). What I have seen Jonathan pursue, embrace, and express are power-packed messages from God that ignite real transformation in our lives, our families, our ministries, and our cultures. This book is one such message.

The most important prophetic word—the one that has become the focal point of Jonathan's ministry—is the Gospel. You may not think of the Gospel as being prophetic, but what could be more prophetic than the Word of God made flesh! (See John 1:14.) Jonathan's passion in all things has been to see people having real encounters with Jesus—ones in which the Gospel deeply impacts and transforms the heart. My own life and ministry have been influenced for the better by Jonathan's example of prioritizing the Gospel. Many times, as someone has described to him a wild spiritual experience they had, I have known Jonathan to ask, "That's great. How does this experience change your life?" If an encounter doesn't bring a deeper application of the Gospel—if it doesn't make us more in love with Jesus or more like Jesus in some way—then it isn't an encounter worth having. Jonathan shows what it looks like to value transformative, Gospel-centric encounters with the living God.

In this book you will read much of Jonathan's own story of transformation. Revelation 12:11 tells us that the proclamation of our testimonies is one of the things that in the end will overcome Satan himself. And in Revelation 19:10 we learn that "the testimony of Jesus is the spirit of prophecy." All prophecy is first Jesus' testimony, and on the other side of the coin, all true testimonies of His work are in some way prophetic. While Scripture is the only unquestionable word of God and the final authority on Jesus's life and who God is, Jesus did not stop working when He left this earth. Rather He continues to act today, and our testimonies are the prophetic declarations of what He is still doing in recent history. What Jesus has done before, He will do again. As you read Jonathan's story, you're actually reading a continuation of Jesus' story. Be encouraged that this same powerful Jesus is mighty to save, heal, and deliver today; and He will act in your life as well.

Prophetic Transformation isn't just another book about prophecy. In fact it has little, if anything, to do with prophetic ministry. More accurately, this text is a look at how the living and active word of the Lord can penetrate to the depths of you and set you free to live like Jesus.

Jonathan, more than any other person I know, models what it looks like to proactively engage in the process of being changed into the image and likeness of Jesus. Scripture teaches us that as we behold and contemplate Jesus, we are gradually transformed into His image with ever-increasing measures of His glory. (See 2 Corinthians 3:18.) As you read and behold Jesus' work in Jonathan's life, expect Jesus to do the same things in you. Expect Him to do the same things *through* you. What Jesus has accomplished in Jonathan, He wants to accomplish in others.

World transformation always begins with personal transformation. As Jesus changes your heart and brings you deeper into alignment with His own, you will become a more accurate prophetic mouthpiece for the Lord, for "out of the overflow of the heart, the mouth speaks." (See Luke 6:45.)

It is my joy to recommend this book to you. When we both reach the other side of eternity, I can't wait to hear your own testimony of what Jesus has done; and I pray a significant portion of your story is traced to the time spent reading and applying this book's message. Jesus is alive, and He has so much more in store for you.

Be blessed,

Art Thomas
Missionary-Evangelist
Wildfire Ministries International

INTRODUCTION

As I was falling asleep a few years ago, the Holy Spirit asked me, "Do you want to have a vision?" I don't remember the Holy Spirit ever asking that before, and He hasn't asked me that since, but that question lives in the heart of God. Do you want to see? Do you want to hear?

I pulled myself out of slumber and said, "Yes."

A brilliant white knight, glowing with the radiance of God's glory, captured my mind's eye. His eyes were like fire. His hands were coated in fire, and he wielded a sword. I somehow knew that I was seeing a spiritual reflection of myself.

God's Word, both in Scripture and in prophetic revelation, is meant to show us who we are—to reveal our identities as sons and daughters of God. James writes that anyone who hears the word and does not do it is like a man who looks at himself in the mirror and then walks away, forgetting what he looks like (James 1:22-25). The purpose of the mirror is not to reveal dirt. The mirror reveals identity. God's Word and revelation—God's voice—reveals who we are. It reveals our identities in Christ.

God intends us to live our lives from that revelation. We become doers of that Word. We put that God-given and God-revealed identity into action. The vision of purity, fire, and knighthood challenges me constantly. I know that this can only be who I am by the great grace and redemption of Jesus Christ. I pray the same will happen for you as you read the coming chapters.

This book is about how experiencing God's voice reveals who we are in Christ to correct us, transform us, and empower us to live holy lives.

I have not lived an exceptionally pure life. I have been shaken by the fear of the Lord more than any Christian should have to because I have often been disobedient to the revelation of holiness that the Lord has already poured into my life. I have misheard God's voice. I have made mistakes. I have received correction and kept moving forward in God's love and discipline. I am thankful for the grace of God and the power of the blood of Christ.

The Bible says that no weapon formed against us shall prosper. My friend Art Thomas likes to add, "Until it gets into my hand as a testimony—then it will prosper against all the work of the enemy."

The weapons that the enemy once used against us become testimonies we wield to take down his strongholds in the lives of others. We overcome by the blood of the Lamb and the word of our testimony (Revelation 12:11), and it is the word of our testimony that carries such power to set others free. The testimonies of who I've been and what I've been through are the inspiration and illustration for this book.

When I started writing, I looked around at the piles of books in my house and asked God, "Do You really need another book?" I asked God to give me a book that no one else could write. This prayer resulted in something deeply personal and a message that intertwines with my life and story.

I have often experienced growth the hard way. My transformation and walk into maturity with God has been full of growing pains. And God's redemptive plan is working to turn those experiences into weapons of purity to wield against the work of the enemy. My prayer is that my life will be a prophetic ladder of sorts—something constructed by Jesus to help others climb out of the pit and out of dangerous places to a place of encounter with the highest Love. I have this hope because God specializes in redeeming failure.

Transformation and repentance are inseparable. My transformation story is also a story of repentance—turning away from darkness and walking into the light, moving from glory to glory, allowing God to change my heart and mind. Because this is a book about transformation, it is also a book about repentance.

I trust God to use my experiences to illustrate His transforming work in our lives. These experiences don't determine my theology, but they do illustrate it. Sanctification, transformation, and the process of God making us like Himself is inextricably linked to our relationship with Jesus.

A book will not enable you to live a holy life unless the Holy Spirit uses it to draw you into the Father's embrace. My prayer is that this book will do that.

We relate to God through communication—hearing Him and responding. Many of the ways God speaks are labeled as "prophetic," and I will use that term often. "Prophetic" means of, or relating to, divine revelation and communication. Any genuine part of our relationship with Jesus is "prophetic." We are immersed in the Spirit, and He is always speaking. We have the mind of Christ, and it is overflowing with precious thoughts for us, more numerous than the grains of sand on the seashore (Psalm 139). We are the sons of God, and we are led by the Spirit (Romans 8:14).

Our circumstances are prophetic. Our interactions with the world are prophetic. Our daily life is prophetic. We may not always recognize it. We may not always turn aside to see the wonder of the burning bush like Moses did. We may not always hear God speaking. But He is speaking. God is surrounding us in revelation. He is surrounding us with His voice.

Prophecy can be defined as saying what God says by God's Spirit. This can refer to the past, present, or the future. It can be personal or "corporate" (meaning for a group of people). It can be general or specific. First Corinthians 14—a very practical chapter on prophecy— teaches, "he who prophesies speaks edification and exhortation and comfort to men" (1 Corinthians 14:3).

Revelation 19:10b states, "For the testimony of Jesus is the spirit of prophecy." Prophecy contains Jesus' testimony. It reveals Him and His message.

As we listen to and walk with Him, we partake of His divine nature (2 Peter 1:4). As we gaze into His glory, we become more like Him. The prophetic purifies. The voice of God calls us out of sin and into holiness. It pushes us into maturity. It speaks a word of faith to our hearts. "Faith comes by hearing and hearing by the word of God" (Romans 10:17). As we hear God's voice, we believe. As we believe, we receive His work and His nature.

This book is not a practical manual on the prophetic, though there are many practical lessons to help you hear God more clearly and accurately. The prophetic should be part of every believer's growth, maturity, and transformation. This book is to a prophetic people and a prophetic Church.

While we are all gifted differently according to God's will, we all have the ability to access all of the Spirit's gifts according to His will and our faith. Visions, dreams, words of knowledge, prophecy, and prophetic experiences are available to all (1 Corinthians 14:31). An analogy I frequently use is that, if asked, each of us could draw a picture of a house. At the very least, we could draw a box with a triangle on top and a window. Some would be able to draw something much more beautiful. Some of us would be gifted. Among the gifted, some would have developed their gift further than others. The same is true of spiritual gifts. If you have never heard God in the ways described in this book, I hope it encourages you that you can.

Receiving certain kinds of revelation does not make you special, and it does not make you holy. It isn't even evidence of a holy life. God's gifts and His call are irrevocable (Romans 11:29 NIV). You don't need a certain experience to be transformed. You don't need experiences similar to mine or anyone else's. You simply need to hear God's Word and obey.

This book is not a practical how-to-stop-sinning-and-be-holy manual. As much as I tried during my early Christian years to find the secret algorithm to holy living, my ultimate revelation was not a pattern of steps or even principles but the person of Jesus Christ and walking with Him.

God's truth gives principles and practical steps we can take within this faith-covenant and relationship with God. I hope this book will be highly practical for everyone who reads it. Even more than that I hope it will make you fall more in love with Jesus—a love so great and furious it burns sin out of your life and gives you a fire you can spread throughout the world. I hope it sets a fire in your heart and holds up a mirror of revelation before your spiritual eyes so that you can gaze into the glory of what it is to be a child of God. I pray you will fully engage in this relationship with Jesus and walk away obedient to the revelation of love that you have seen in Him.

God's desire is to multiply His glory and image throughout the earth through His Church. The process we go through of conforming to His glory and being changed by God's Word is often called sanctification. But this is more than a mechanical process. It is a series of experiences with the person of Jesus. It is a relationship. It is a relationship of revelation. It is a relationship full of prophetic experiences that transform our lives.

This book is about moving deeper and deeper into both the prophetic experiences and the holiness that God has for us. Through His voice, God changes us from glory to glory.

ACTION STEP

Every chapter in this book ends with an action step. This is a practical exercise designed to help you receive revelation and transformation. These steps are not an algorithm for hearing God, receiving repentance, or being transformed. They are simply tools to help you hear God and respond to His Word.

Often the action steps exist to distill a simple act of obedience from Scripture. Still more often, they prompt "listening-prayer" by giving simple questions to ask God.

You don't have to stop and go through the action steps at the end of each chapter. You can read the book through and then go back to them. I do encourage you to go through each one of them. I did as I wrote them, and as a result I had a number of profound moments with God.

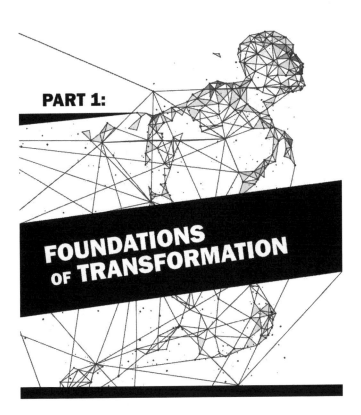

PART 1:

FOUNDATIONS OF TRANSFORMATION

The *Turritopsis dohrnii* jellyfish drifts through the ocean with an effervescent glow. Scientists are still investigating the complex beauty of this creation. They are fascinated by God's unique design of this specific jellyfish.

The *Turritopsis dohrnii* is able to grow younger and begin its life cycle again and again. Like a caterpillar transforming into a butterfly, the Jellyfish transforms from a polyp until it reaches the complex and beautiful form with which we are most familiar. But it never loses its ability to change. The *Turritopsis dohrnii* or "Immortal Jellyfish" can regenerate back into a polyp and become new again and again (Rich).

While Scientists examine the "Immortal Jellyfish" searching for the secret of immortality, I am reminded of God's design—His redemption in our lives, how He endlessly cleanses and renews, and how He has given us the ability to change in response to His voice.

The Immortal Jellyfish transforms in response to its environment. The Holy Spirit within us enables us to change in response to God's voice. We were designed to hear the voice of God and respond.

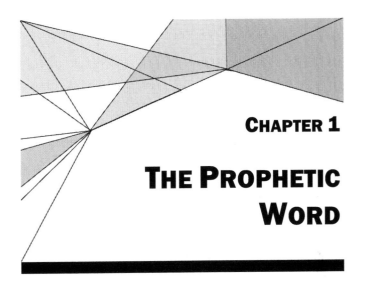

CHAPTER 1

THE PROPHETIC WORD

My head spun as I stood in my freshman dorm. I was hearing voices. Repetitive, tormenting voices on the edge of incoherence crowded out my own thoughts and brought with them a nearly paralyzing sense of despair. The years previous had included cutting and burning myself, pledging myself to Satan, and fantasizing about being one of the soldiers who tortured Jesus on the cross; but I had never felt that I was out of control.

Now I knew I was out of control.

I was terrified of losing my mind. I got down on my knees and told the God I hated, "I will do whatever You want if You take these voices out of my head."

There is much more of this story to tell, but to put it simply: God heard my cry. He took the voices away, and He spoke to me that night.

I didn't know what to do. I remember going to bed wondering whether God had really spoken to me. I was confused.

I felt the intense grip of a hand on the inside. I knew that I had to make a choice. Would I believe that the God of the entire universe—whom I had hated and blasphemed for so long—had just answered my prayer and spoken to me? All I knew was that I couldn't hear the voices, and I didn't care about the despair or hopelessness. I was consumed with the question of what to do with this encounter with God.

I lay awake all night. I saw memory after memory pass before my eyes. All the determining events of my life came to the surface and were peeled away like layers. With the removal of each one came a stripping away of emotion and motivation. When I got out of bed in the morning, I did not know who I was. The hand on the inside had not released its grip, and I knew that I had to do something.

The only thought I could hold onto was that I had to pray with someone. I had met the campus pastor months earlier, so I went to his office and told him the story of what had happened. I'm sure it was far less articulate than I have explained it here. I was walking in a haze. I felt that my identity had been stolen. I didn't know who I was, and even more frightening— I no longer felt any of the motivations or desires that had driven my life before. What remained was a sense of blankness and loss combined with an overwhelming conviction that I had gotten everything wrong.

I prayed a simple prayer with the campus pastor, a man who would go on to love and care for me more than almost anyone else in my life.

He told me, "The angels in heaven are rejoicing."

I thought, *The angels may be rejoicing, but I am confused.* I

walked back to my dorm room in a daze and sat on the
edge of my bed. I looked around the room at my books,
movies, music, and posters. I was overwhelmed with grief.
Everything in my life, all that I had loved, seemed evil. It
was all pain, darkness, and anger. I thought, *I can't do those
things anymore. What do Christians do? Well, Christians read the
Bible.* So I went on a hunt to find the King James Bible my
parents had given me for Christmas one year.

Someone somewhere had said that First John was a
good book for new Christians to read. I flipped the pages
until I found First John. I started to read, and word after
word pounded nails into my heart. "God is light and in
Him is no darkness at all. If we say that we have fellowship
with Him and walk in darkness, we lie and do not practice
the truth" (1 John 1:5-6).

My insides were screaming. I looked around my
room again. All that I loved was darkness. I had walked in
darkness for years. This was not making me feel better.
"Do not love the world or the things in the world. If
anyone loves the world the love of the Father is not in
him" (1 John 2:15). All that I had loved was the world. All
that I cared about was the things of the world. I was
overwhelmed with grief. How could I do this? I was so
evil. My life was so evil. I put the Bible down. This didn't
seem to be helping; I only felt worse.

I thought, *What else do Christians do? They praise God.* I
went to my computer, found some worship music, and
started to play it. I listened to the voices praising and
worshipping God for His goodness, love, grace, and glory.
I couldn't understand it. *How can I praise God when all I can
see or feel is my sin?* I couldn't be a Christian this way. I said
out loud, "God if You want me to do this, You're going to

have to fill me with something."

In an instant everything changed. I cannot adequately describe the incredible love—pure, flowing, selfless, joyful—that flooded me. I wept and spread my arms wide. I stood there and loved and loved and loved.

And God loved me.

It was the most profound moment of my life, and it still is. The memory alone stirs me. I never recovered. It was like a switch had flipped on the inside. It made no sense; no one explained it to me. It went past understanding. God loved me, and I loved Him. In spite of all that I had been and done, God loved me, accepted me, called out to me, answered me, filled me, and wanted me. God loved. I came alive on the inside.

I look back, and I am so grateful for the story of God's great love and redemption in my life. The chronology doesn't make sense, and it may not follow the pattern of salvation in a systematic theology, but it is the greatest thing that God has ever done in my life. The way He did it has shaped my interactions with Him.

First John remains my favorite epistle and is the book of the Bible I have read the most. I'm trying to memorize it now, reciting its chapters over and over again, reminding myself of the words that struck my soul on that day the love of God flooded my heart. I didn't make it to the words of First John Chapter Four that day, but I experienced them in the Holy Spirit: "God is love."

The Bible is the Word of God. It leads us into an experience with Him, and it keeps us safe in that experience. Without the conviction and the plain truth of First John 1-3, I don't think my salvation story would be the same. The words jumped off the page to me. They struck my heart in a unique way. Reading them for the first time with the Holy Spirit forever shaped the way I see the world, myself, and the love of God. First John wasn't something that passed me by or that I didn't understand when I read it; it was alive.

Many may wonder how God spoke to me the night before or be amazed at the eighteen hours of memories and conviction. They might ask about what I prayed with my campus pastor or talk about what happened when I told God that He had to fill me with something if I was going to be able to do what He wanted. All those things are precious to me, but apart from that moment when Jesus stepped into my heart and brought His love, the moment I revisit the most is that first time I read First John.

I relive it again and again because I read First John again and again, and I hear God's Words jump off the page again and again. Scripture led me into the experience I had with Jesus. It provided an arrow to the heart of God. I found God's heart because Scripture pointed me there.

Scripture reveals the mystery of the Gospel: We have a basis for a relationship with God because Jesus Christ died on the cross and shed His blood for the forgiveness of our sins. Then He rose from the dead so that we could have a new life in fellowship with Him. Jesus removed the enmity caused by sin. He did away with the bad relationship we'd had with God because of the disobedience of the human race and our own individual disobedience, and He restored us to a right relationship with our heavenly Father. When we receive this truth and surrender to Jesus as our Lord and Master, we have the basis for a good relationship with God—a series of experiences with the Person of God.

Peter wrote:

> **2 Peter 1:16-21 –** For we did not follow cleverly devised myths when we made known to you the power and coming of our Lord Jesus Christ, but we were eyewitnesses of His majesty. For when He received honor and glory from God the Father, and the voice was borne to Him by the Majestic Glory, "This is my beloved Son, with whom I am well pleased," we ourselves heard this very voice borne from heaven, for we were with Him on the holy mountain. And we have the prophetic word more fully confirmed, to which you will do well to pay attention as to a lamp shining in a dark place, until the day dawns and the morning star rises in your hearts, knowing this first of all, that no prophecy of Scripture comes from someone's own interpretation. For no prophecy was ever produced by the will of man, but men spoke from God as they were carried along by the Holy Spirit.

Peter wrote to the Church that he and the other Apostles did not follow made-up stories. Rather, they knew, saw, and experienced Jesus. They were present at the Transfiguration and heard God speak from heaven, "This is my beloved Son in whom I am well pleased." This must have been a life-changing event. They spent years with Jesus, but now they saw Him glorified with their physical eyes, and they heard God speak audibly with their physical ears. There could be no greater proof, no more certain empirical evidence, no greater basis for their faith. They had a physical experience with the revelation of Jesus and the audible voice of God.

But Peter wrote that there is a greater proof—a more-certain evidence and a greater basis for faith. There is a greater prophetic Word. The word they heard from heaven, spoken directly from God in an audible way, was a less-sure prophetic word. The most-sure prophetic Word is Scripture.

Peter continued that this sure prophetic Word is meant for all of us and provided by the Holy Spirit, not by man. Scripture is God's will given a voice.

Only Jesus and the Holy Spirit surpass Scripture's ability to reveal Father God. Yet Scripture is the prophetic Word by which we measure every other revelation. It is the standard. It is the measuring stick and the plumb line. Scripture leads us, guides us, and protects us as we experience God and His voice in other ways. The Bible is the objective, certain, sure, reliable Word of God, and the revelation of His will.

If we want to hear and be transformed by God's voice, we must saturate ourselves in the biblical revelation. If we want to know what God sounds like, we can grow accustomed to His voice in the pages of Scripture. If we want to experience Him, we can with the prophets in the pages of Scripture, and this Word is made alive through the power of the Holy Spirit. If we have access to Scripture and do not attempt to fill our lives with this Word, we are not genuinely trying to hear God's voice. At any given moment, we are as close to prophetic revelation as we are to a Bible. We can open the Bible and have an experience with God's Word today, right now, and that is nothing to take lightly.

I desire to have perfect prophetic experiences with God every single day, but I must admit that outside of daily Bible reading, I don't. I want to hear God's voice perfectly, but I have heard God incorrectly many times. I have never regretted hearing God in Scripture. I can study Scripture incorrectly. I can apply Scripture incorrectly. I can interpret Scripture incorrectly. But if I am reading the Bible with an open heart, I can be certain that I am in the correct place to receive a word from God.

The Bible is the place to start for every believer desiring to hear the voice of God. If we approach the Bible with faith we will never be disappointed. This prophetic Word still speaks and always will. We are a people of one book, and there is no way to get to the bottom of it. There is always more to hear from the Holy Spirit in the pages of the Bible.

Paul instructed his son in the faith Timothy:

2 Timothy 3:16-17 – All Scripture is given by inspiration of God, and is profitable for doctrine, for reproof, for correction, for instruction in righteousness, that the man of God may be complete, thoroughly equipped for every good work.

This book is not only about hearing God's voice but also how God's voice changes us. If we want to be transformed, changed, sanctified, and perfected, we must look to Scripture. More than any prophetic experience apart from salvation, Scripture is guaranteed to transform your life. Day by day, verse by verse, Scripture will teach you.

Through the words of Scripture the Holy Spirit will correct and reprove you. The words of Scripture will instruct you in righteous living. The prophetic word of Scripture has the power to equip you in every way you need and to complete you in Christ. That is an incredible promise. It may seem too good to be true, but this Scripture doesn't say you need a vision or a dream, a prophetic word or an audible voice. It says that the Holy Spirit speaking through Scripture purposes to complete God's work in you and to give you what you need for every good work.

This book is based on Scripture, and Scripture itself commands us to hear God's voice through the ministry of the Holy Spirit, who works and manifests Himself in many different ways. God's voice is speaking right now in various ways, and they are all available to us. We must not be deaf to them. When we neglect Scripture, we neglect the voice of God and the Holy Spirit.

If you want prophetic transformation in your life, know that it is guaranteed and given to you in the pages of the Bible. The Bible may not tell you which job to take or where to live, though it certainly has wisdom on those topics, but it can tell you how to be changed into the likeness of Christ and how to live a holy life. We must hear, study, and devour the whole of God's truth. We renew our minds in the written Word; we also listen for the presently-spoken word from God's Spirit.

There are believers all over the world who do not have access to the Bible for various reasons. They must rely on the Holy Spirit alone to hear God. They don't have the option to hear God's voice without judging and testing the revelation. We, however, have a prophetic Word available to us that is tested and tried. It is true. You can hear it without reservation. The Bible remains the starting place for prophetic transformation. It stands as the standard and foundation for hearing the voice of God. Hearing God's voice can be as simple as opening the Bible with a heart that says, "Speak Lord, your servant is listening."

ACTION STEP

Are you saturating your life with Scripture?

Take one minute to meditate with the Holy Spirit on what kind of Bible reading habits He wants in your life. What does this look like daily? Weekly? Monthly?

Suggested Goal: The Cornerstone Reading Plan

"Now, therefore, you are no longer strangers and foreigners, but fellow citizens with the saints and members of the household of God, having been built on the foundation of the apostles and prophets, Jesus Christ Himself being the chief cornerstone." (Ephesians 2:19-20)

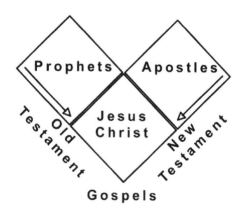

A cornerstone is the first stone laid in a building project and determines the angles and direction for the rest of the building. Jesus Christ is the cornerstone and a great place to start a reading plan.

1. The Gospels

You can start by reading one chapter per day in the book of Matthew.

After you feel comfortable reading one chapter per day and have success, you can start adding the New Testament writings of the Apostles, starting with the book of Acts.

2. The New Testament

Now you are reading two chapters per day, one in the Gospels and one in the rest of the New Testament. After you are comfortable with that and are having success, you can add the Old Testament books, written by the prophets, starting with Genesis.

3. The Old Testament

After success with that, you can add a chapter in the Old Testament, starting with the book of Psalms. This results in reading four chapters per day. After you finish the Book of John in the Gospels, you can cycle back to Matthew, and after you finish the book of Revelation in the New Testament, you can cycle back to the book of Acts.

If you follow this plan for fifteen months you will read through the Old Testament once, the New Testament two and a half times and the Gospels five times. This is a good place to start in saturating yourself with God's word. Remember to listen and obey as you read.

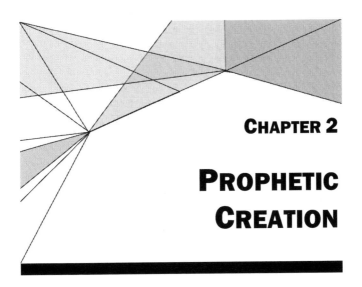

CHAPTER 2

PROPHETIC CREATION

Genesis 1:1 – In the beginning God created the heavens and the earth.

God is the great Creator, Initiator, Life-Giver, and Origin. All things are derived as a response to Him who was and is and is to come. He is the Eternal, Almighty God, and at His Word something came out of nothing.

The Spirit of God hovered over the surface of the deep, and out of God's great imagination came the Words, "Let there be light." What was once empty and formless was filled with light at the sound of His Word.

John 1:1,3 – In the beginning was the Word, and the Word was with God and the Word was God. All things were made by Him and without Him was not anything made that was made.

When God looked at His original creation, He saw

that it was good. The land and water, the grass and trees and vegetation, seeds and fruit were all "good" in God's eyes (Genesis 1:12). Night and day, the sun, stars and moon and all the seasons were "good" in God's eyes. All the creatures in the sea and all the birds of the air were "good" and blessed by God. The animals on the land were "good" and blessed by God. Humanity, made in the image of God, was evaluated in the balance of creation as "very good" and was blessed by God.

God was not afraid to call His creation "good" because it stood as a perfect response to His voice and His Spirit. It perfectly reflected and represented who He was. Creation accurately showed His infinite goodness and grace. It rang out with a clear, perfect tone the great song of God's heart. It shone with the beauty of His radiance. It danced to the rhythm of His heart. It was a world of worship.

The original creation was a world where God's voice was heard in every living thing. Every fish in the sea swam with the motion that God's Word had given it. Every leaf on every tree held the shape and color that God's Word had given it. The sun, moon, and stars all shone with the brilliance and purity of God's spoken Word. Man and woman lived and breathed in perfect union with the Word of God who created them. His infinite kindness and love was written on the face of every created thing, and every created thing resembled this love.

In a world where all things spoke with the clear voice of God, humanity spoke a clearer word of who God was. We were made preeminent over all of creation. We were His masterpiece—the part of creation that most fully carried His voice and His Word. We brought a part of

Him into substance that no other part of creation could. We carried a fullness of His image that no other part of creation could carry. We lived in a relationship with Him that was on a completely different level than the rest of creation. We responded to God, expressed God, and demonstrated God in a way that made the angels and participants in the spiritual realms gaze and wonder.

We had a perfect relationship with God. We walked and talked with Him in the cool of the day. In a universe of responses to the voice of God, ours was perfect.

The original creation paralleled heaven in its expression of God. God's will was done perfectly. God's voice was heard clearly. God was worshiped fully by all things. Anywhere and everywhere you looked, you could see God.

Part of our internal makeup as human beings includes the instinct that we should be able to see and experience God through creation and through each other. We were designed to look for God in each other. We have a hunger to seek God in this world because God's original design spoke of Him so accurately that we felt no distance from Him. His voice was everywhere. His Word was everywhere. Every glance of our eyes was saturated with a display of God's nature. When Adam looked at Eve and when Eve looked at Adam, there was a deep exchange of the revelation of the goodness and love of God.

Now all of creation has been affected by sin and the fall of man. The once-clear calling of God in every piece of matter only remains as a faint echo. But even a faint echo of God can be transforming and illuminating.

Paul wrote, "For since the creation of the world [God's] invisible attributes are clearly seen, being understood by the things that are made, even His eternal power and Godhead" (Romans 1:20). God's attributes, which we cannot see with our natural eyes, are still clearly seen and experienced in natural creation. The voice of God still speaks through nature, communicating His identity and character to all who will listen.

When we gaze into the starry sky or at the vastness of the ocean we are given a clear view of the eternal power of God. Gazing into a microscope at the infinite complexity of a single cell or far past our galaxy through the Hubble Space Telescope at the infinite distance of outer space helps us understand the eternal power of God. Creation still testifies of an eternal God who loves and cares for us.

INTIMACY WITH GOD

We originally lived in a world that was perfectly pleasing to God, and we perfectly pleased God by simply being what we were made to be. We walked in a unique faith relationship with God that was natural to us from the very beginning. "But without faith it is impossible to please Him, for he who comes to God must believe that He is, and that He is a rewarder of those who diligently seek Him" (Hebrews 11:6). We pleased God perfectly as we communed perfectly with His spoken Word. We trusted explicitly that God was and that God was a rewarder. We believed in Him because we saw a perfect expression of Him everywhere. We believed in His goodness because His goodness was in full manifestation all around us.

Our original faith-covenant with God was established by His Word and command to us as His children:

> **Genesis 2:16-17 –** And the LORD God
> commanded the man, saying, "Of every tree of
> the garden you may freely eat, but of the tree of
> knowledge of good and evil you shall not eat, for
> in the day you eat of it you shall surely die."

We were free to eat from every tree, including the Tree of Life at the center of the garden (Genesis 2:9). This was the divine covenant God gave to us and that we were meant to fulfill by faith. By seeking God and following His voice, humanity was meant to come to the center of the garden and eat of the tree of life. We were meant to respond to God's great love by diligently seeking Him and receiving the reward of eternal life there at the center of the garden in the midst of intimacy with God.

Within this world of worship, intimacy was still a necessity. There remained degrees of relationship and response to God. There was work to be done—a calling and a vocation to fulfill. There was also a time to be intimate with God—to walk with Him in the cool of the day and to respond to the unique calling of His voice. This intimacy was a higher response to God and His Spirit and the most precious moment of fellowship between God and man. The opportunity for this highest response to God and His love was where the first evidence of humanity's fall appeared. Intimacy was broken.

TEMPTATION AND FALL

We received "the knowledge of good and evil" by breaking the divine covenant with God and disobeying his expressed command. "Like Adam, they have broken the covenant—they were unfaithful to me there" (Hosea 6:7).

Our unfaithfulness resulted in opening a new realm to us—the knowledge of evil.

While immersed in a world transmitting the unmuted voice of God, we chose to doubt God and respond to the voice of the devil. We doubted first His Word (Genesis 3:1-4) and then His goodness (Genesis 3:5), denying all of creation's testimony and draw. We fell from our original identity and marred the image of God.

Our thoughts and focus turned from God to our own nakedness (Genesis 3:7). Our intimacy with God was ruined as we descended into confusion, guilt, and futility of mind, attempting to hide from God and avoid His voice. We were banished from the place of fellowship with God—barred and cut off from the Tree of Life and separated from God in spiritual death. Our complete freedom to respond to God was lost to bondage. Rebellion against God tuned our nature to the sound of sin instead of the voice of God.

When humanity fell, the entire world fell with us. "The heaven, even the heavens, are the LORD's; But the earth He has given to the children of men" (Psalm 115:16). The authority and dominion that God gave us over all of creation meant that sin passed through us to the whole world (Rom 5:12).

Even as our image and representation of God became marred, all of the world's witness to the Creator became skewed. Where God's will was once plainly expressed, sin, pain, and death now dominate. The original lies that Satan spoke to Eve infected the entire world system. Where circumstances, events, creation, and humanity once hummed with the voice of Love, they now bear a false witness, casting doubt on God's Word and His goodness. The result of the fall is that God's will is no longer perfectly expressed in the world.

Every day people cry out in pain to God, "Why?" because they suffer the cruelty and death caused by sin. The root of all depression, oppression, sickness, poverty, and death is the presence and authority of sin and the devil in this once-perfect world.

We were designed to see God in one another, to look for divine revelation in those around us. Humanity is heartsick because we look at the unspeakable evil committed in the world today, and we allow what we see to form our perspective of God.

> **1 John 5:19 –** We know that we are of God, and the whole world lies under the sway of the wicked one.

The whole world is under the sway, power, and rule of the devil. Because sin entered the world, each of us was born corrupted. Satan enslaved the world to sin.

> **John 8:34 –** "Jesus answered them, 'Most assuredly, I say to you, whoever commits sin is a slave of sin.'"

The whole world lives as slaves of the devil, yet people were made to rule, made for love, and made to possess God-breathed Life. They live addicted and enslaved, afraid and alone, bitter, wounded, "foolish, disobedient, deceived, serving various lusts and pleasures, living in malice and envy, hateful and hating one another" (Titus 3:2)—a tortured existence without God and without hope. "But when the kindness and love of God our Savior

41

toward man appeared…" He saved us (Titus 3:3).

This is the wonderful Good News, the appearance of the kindness and love of God our Savior. Jesus, the kindness and love of God in human flesh, came not to destroy men's lives but to save them (Luke 9:56).

> **1 John 3:8 –** "For this purpose the Son of God was manifested, that He might destroy the works of the devil."

Jesus was manifested; He appeared in kindness and love to destroy the yoke of slavery, to demolish the rule of the devil over man, and to save us from sin and evil. Jesus came to give us abundant life in the love and favor of the Father.

Though the devil rules this world for a time, Jesus has defeated the power of death and has risen to obtain a name above every name that at the name of Jesus every knee will bow and every tongue confess that Christ is Lord (Philippians 2:10-11). All authority has been given to the Lord Jesus (Matthew 28:18); and at the end of time, He will come as the King of Kings and Lord of Lords, giving justice to all who rejected His love and lordship. Even now He waits, not willing that any should perish under His justice but giving all men time to turn and come under the rule of love (2 Peter 3:9).

Satan rules over this world (1 John 5:19, Ephesians 2:2). God rules over us. We hear His voice, obey His Word, and spread His rule and reign.

CREATED TO HEAR

You were created to hear God's voice. You were

designed from the beginning to have a unique fellowship with God that displays His love and glory. This means that your body, soul, and spirit were intended to commune with God. They were created to experience God. In the fall, we lost much of what God intended, but our internal makeup is still based on the purpose of interacting with God.

Hearing God's voice is natural. It is part of who we are as human beings. Hearing and fellowshipping with God means fulfilling our internal and external design. Your mind was created ideal for hearing God. Your soul was created ideal for hearing God. Your spirit was designed ideal for hearing God. Your body was created ideal for hearing God.

We often denigrate or dismiss what seems natural or normal as not being from God. But if we were designed for fellowship, then hearing God's voice should seem natural. In fact, when voices came from the sky and extreme external circumstances occurred, there was often confusion. The Israelites feared God when He displayed His glory on the mountain (Exodus 20:19-20). The crowds before Jesus disbelieved and rationalized even when an external voice came from heaven (John 12:28-29). Elijah found that God was not in the earthquake or the whirlwind or the fire. Elijah heard God in a still, small voice—a low, quiet whisper (1 Kings 19:11-13).

To hear God's voice well, we must acknowledge the small and the natural—the low, quiet whispers in life. Moses turned aside for a bush that was on fire in the desert. This was not unusual. But as he watched it, it wasn't burning up. That didn't seem quite right. When he approached the bush, he had a supernatural encounter.

We must turn aside for the small promptings of God's voice in order to hear and fellowship with Him. We can't dismiss the small cues and the natural experiences we have. We have to acknowledge God's presence and design in all of creation—including ourselves.

THE IMAGINATION

Matthew 5:27-28 – "You have heard that it was said to those of old, 'You shall not commit adultery.' But I say to you that whoever looks at a woman to lust for her has already committed adultery with her in his heart."

God takes our imaginations seriously. Our thoughts and fantasies can lead us into ungodliness. They can be sin. Jesus equated the act of adultery in the heart and imagination with the actual act. This does not mean that any passing thought of adultery makes you guilty, but that the active desire and fantasy of adultery does. What you deliberately do in your mind is connected to your heart and impacts your holiness. God takes it seriously.

Many believers take the imagination seriously when it comes to sin and fantasy but immediately dismiss it when it comes to fellowship with God. God did not design our imagination for sin. God did not design our imagination to lead us into ungodliness. God designed our imagination for fellowship with Him. He designed our imagination to lead us into holiness.

God created part of our brain to see and make mental pictures, and He wants to speak to us through that part of our brain. Jeremiah's introduction to his calling serves as an introduction to the prophetic, which God preserved for all of us:

> **Jeremiah 1:2-10 –** Then the word of the Lord
> came to me, saying: "Before I formed you in the
> womb I knew you; Before you were born I
> sanctified you; I ordained you a prophet to the
> nations."
>
> Then said I: "Ah, Lord God! Behold, I cannot
> speak, for I am a youth."
>
> But the Lord said to me: "Do not say, 'I am a
> youth,' For you shall go to all to whom I send
> you, And whatever I command you, you shall
> speak. Do not be afraid of their faces, For I am
> with you to deliver you," says the Lord.
>
> Then the Lord put forth His hand and
> touched my mouth, and the Lord said to me:
> "Behold, I have put My words in your mouth.
> See, I have this day set you over the nations and
> over the kingdoms, To root out and to pull
> down, To destroy and to throw down, To build
> and to plant."

God formed Jeremiah in the womb and set him apart before his birth to be a prophet to the nations. This was part of God's design for Jeremiah's personality, gifting, and calling. We are all designed differently, and we all experience and fellowship with God in unique ways. Jeremiah's calling and gifting resulted in a relationship with God that included visions, spontaneous prophetic words, written prophetic words, prophetic actions, and more. And this had little to do with his holiness or maturity. He was a young man. God did not care about his age. God cared about the purpose for which he was created.

Jeremiah was a prophet, and we are a prophetic community. God's Spirit is no longer poured out on only a few "called" individuals but on all flesh (Acts 2:16-17). Every son and daughter will prophesy. Instead of one voice leading God's people, God has endowed His whole community with His Spirit. Every believer hears God's voice. Every believer has discernment. The community as a whole hears God's voice and judges revelation.

You may not be called or gifted like Jeremiah, but you can hear the voice of God. You have the same Spirit that Jeremiah had. You were also designed to hear God's voice and for that voice to lead you into holiness.

Jeremiah 1:11 – Moreover the word of the Lord came to me, saying, "Jeremiah, what do you see?"

The Word of the Lord came to Jeremiah, but he didn't recount how. I think the Bible often avoids giving specifics of how God speaks to keep us from making strange doctrines or rules about hearing God's voice.

We must be open to any number of ways that the Lord chooses to communicate. In this case, it could have been an external voice. It could have been an internal voice. It could have been a still, small voice or a "thought in the heart." This word prompted Jeremiah to see something. God asked, "Jeremiah, what do you see?" God asks questions to draw us into conversation with Him. God also prompted Jeremiah to hear His voice in a new way.

I wonder what was going through Jeremiah's head at that moment. It is possible that he immediately went into a vision that he saw with his open eyes. However, God's question makes me wonder if the vision was less obvious than that. Maybe Jeremiah thought, Oh wait, I'm supposed to see something? Blink, blink. I don't see anything. Well, God said I was supposed to see something. Maybe I should look again in a different way.

I have had visions that overwhelmed my physical eyes, but most often I have visions when my eyes are closed. They occur in my imagination or in the part of my mind that God created to make pictures. Clearly, not everything we imagine is from God, but God can inspire pictures in our mind. We must use our discernment and familiarity with our Father to know when God is speaking to us.

I wonder if God asked Jeremiah what he saw because He wanted Jeremiah to pay attention to the mental picture that He was sending. He not only wanted Jeremiah to see something, but to learn how to hear His voice. This conversation in Jeremiah Chapter One was God teaching Jeremiah how to see.

> **Jeremiah 1:11b-12 –** And I said, "I see a branch of an almond tree."
> Then the Lord said to me, "You have seen well, for I am ready to perform My word."

Jeremiah responded by telling the Lord what he sees. God already knew, but God desires relationship. God's response to what Jeremiah saw is revealing, "You have seen well." God affirmed what Jeremiah saw. Jeremiah needed this affirmation. He needed God to say, "That's right; you got it." We also need confirmation for what we see and hear from God. This most often comes from fruit in our lives and the confirmation of God's community around us. This is especially needed when we hear God in new ways or when God's voice is subtle. My experience is that God's voice is often more subtle than we would like and that it pushes us to know Him better and lean more on His Church.

> **Jeremiah 1:13 –** And the word of the Lord came to me the second time, saying, "What do you see?"
> And I said, "I see a boiling pot, and it is facing away from the north."

God initiated a similar conversation a second time; His word came to Jeremiah in some non-visual way, prompting Jeremiah to seek and respond regarding something visual, or a vision, from God. Both times, the image did not initially make sense. It required interpretation. Rather than affirming Jeremiah again, God spoke to the meaning and the fruit of what Jeremiah saw.

> **Jeremiah 1:14-16 –** Then the Lord said to me: "Out of the north calamity shall break forth On all the inhabitants of the land. For behold, I am calling All the families of the kingdoms of the north," says the Lord; "They shall come and each one set his throne At the entrance of the gates of Jerusalem, Against all its walls all around, And against all the cities of Judah. I will utter My judgments Against them concerning all their wickedness, Because they have forsaken Me, Burned incense to other gods, And worshiped the works of their own hands.

This fruit would be confirmed, and Jeremiah's word now stands as Scripture—the prophetic standard. God's word to Jeremiah was meant to lead both Jeremiah and the nation of Israel into holiness and right relationship with Him. God gave this word of judgment to spare Israel punishment.

God speaks to us about who we are in Him, about who we are in His calling, and about our growth and transformation. Some things we experience in our fellowship with God are immediately discernible as safe and fruitful; however, Paul commanded us to test all things:

> **1 Thessalonians 5:20-21** – Do not despise prophecies. Test all things; hold fast what is good.

We must not despise prophecies. We can't treat God's revelation with contempt. We can't be dismissive. We must believe that God does speak to both us and others. Denying this is a symptom of an evil heart of unbelief. Denying that we can make mistakes is gross pride. Paul commanded us to test and judge revelation because we can make mistakes.

In the Old Testament, prophets who erred were to be ignored (Deuteronomy 18:22). Prophets who led the people after false Gods were to be killed (Deuteronomy 13). In the past, a few gifted individuals had the Holy Spirit, so they had to be right for the sake of the whole community.

Now every single believer has a relationship with God, and every single believer has discernment. We judge prophecy. If it's wrong or erroneous, we correct and grow. If it leads to other gods, it is false prophecy, and we expel that person from the community if they do not repent. Whether interpreting Scripture or seeking to hear God's voice, we can make mistakes. God's desire is for us is to learn and grow.

We must desire intimacy and communication with God. This is what we were made for. It is part of how we experience God and His Word. God wants to open our ears and our eyes. He wants us to hear and to hear accurately. He wants to correct us, lead us, and guide us. If we cut ourselves off from God's voice in Scripture or in revelation through His Spirit, we cut ourselves off from transformation.

We still inhabit God's design for a prophetic creation. We are being transformed by His voice and to be His voice to a fallen world. When we enter this relationship, we grow back into what it truly means to be human.

ACTION STEP

➢ What are some ways that you have heard God in the past?

➢ What are some ways God speaks in Scripture that you have not experienced?

➢ Have you heard God's voice in internal words or audio?

➢ Have you heard God's voice through a feeling?

➢ Have you heard God's voice through an internal picture?

➢ What are some ways that you can pray without words?

➢ Take at least five minutes to pray using the Head, Heart, Hands prayer. During the listening time, pay attention to what God is saying and how.

HEAD, HEART, HANDS Prayer

1 Corinthians 14:15

HEAD: What are you thankful for? What do you want to worship God for? What's on your mind? What do you want from God?

HEART: What are you feeling? What's on your heart? Spend time speaking to God without words. Spend time listening to what God says.

HANDS: How will you respond to how God met you in prayer? How will this prayer time change your life? Worship Him for answering the prayer.

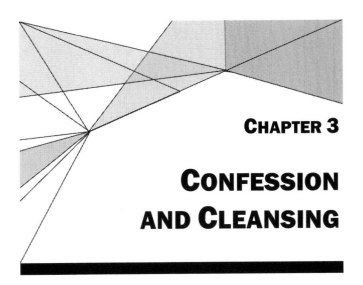

CHAPTER 3

CONFESSION AND CLEANSING

After leading a Bible study with a few Muslim and Hindu men, I returned home to shower, pray, and worship. On Thursday nights I attended a church led by my friend Art Thomas. The fellowship was one of the highlights of my week. Every meeting contained testimonies, miraculous healings, words of knowledge, and prophecy.

This Thursday the Holy Spirit was working in a different way. I was dancing around my apartment singing old choruses and energetically rejoicing. This remains one of the most vital aspects of my life with Jesus. The joy of the Lord is our strength, and His joy was present. I was swept up in the tangible presence and empowering of the Spirit. I couldn't stop singing, laughing, shouting, jumping, and praising God with all my strength. This went on for an hour or two when the moment intensified and shifted. I began singing love songs to Jesus.

It was about twenty minutes before I needed to leave for Art's house when the Holy Spirit put my face in the carpet.

I had felt intense conviction before. It felt like the center of my body was shot through with a fiery current. I also had a deep sense of being caught.

God's conviction comes with a purpose. The Lord never convicts us without putting His finger on the place He wants to cleanse. The enemy often attempts to mimic God's conviction, but he can only condemn. The devil can't inspire change or bring hope of cleansing.

The Holy Spirit does not accuse. He convicts, but even His conviction is not mirrored by earthly conviction. The Holy Spirit doesn't pass sentence on us. He doesn't tell us we are finished. He convinces us that we must change.

Earlier in the week I had a bout of insomnia and in the early hours of the morning, half asleep, I chose lust. I sincerely repented, but these struggles with insomnia and lust had become periodic over the last year. Lying on my face in God's presence I knew that I had allowed lust to place a hook in my heart that needed to be removed.

I had confessed to two brothers in the Lord earlier in the week, yet the Holy Spirit was touching an area where lust still had a hold on my heart. I heard the Lord speak clearly, "Tonight, I want to do a cleansing work." The words were specific to me. Beyond the words I heard inside, I had a sudden knowledge. I was apprehended by fear. I knew God wanted me to publicly confess my sin to the group and open the door for others to do the same.

Two youth leaders attended the Thursday night church, and they had told testimonies of how God was working in their youth group. The leaders had been preparing the youth for a testimony night, when each student would have the opportunity to share about what God was doing in their lives. As they were preparing for the testimony night, God gave a word of knowledge to the leaders that several of the youth were praying for boldness because of what the Lord wanted them to share during the next week. The word of knowledge resulted in a flooded altar call, and the leaders gave up their plans for that night and allowed the Holy Spirit to minister to the hearts of the youth. God prepared them for the coming week.

The next week the testimony night opened with the public confession of sin and struggles as the youth received healing for wounded hearts and freedom from bondage and captivity.

As I lay on my face before the King and Kings, I knew that God wanted to spread what he was doing in that youth group to my life and to the Thursday night church.

I picked myself off the floor and started driving to Art's house, struggling the whole time with the prospect of publicly confessing my sins, specifically lust, to a group of young men and women, who thought highly of me. My pride fought me. I didn't want to expose the sin and weakness in my life.

I prayed during the drive, asking the Lord to provide confirmation and instruction about how I should do this. I didn't want to blurt out my sins at the beginning of the meeting. I didn't want to confess my sins at all. I consecrated my heart in prayer, telling God that I was willing to do whatever He wanted me to do.

When I arrived at Art's house, his power had just gone out. He was busy setting up lanterns and flashlights so we could continue. I sat in the dim light and sang quietly to myself, "Holy Spirit, Thou art welcome…" I talked to Jesus while doodling in my notebook. His still, small voice said, "I want to cleanse the inside of the cup."

The group opened with testimonies and prayer requests, and someone asked for prayer for anxiety. The group began to minister to one another and sharing testimonies of freedom from anxiety and depression.

Art began to teach and prayed for the anxiety to leave. Several people prayed for God's peace to fill the room. As we prayed to receive God's peace, Art continued teaching about intimacy with God and then moved on to what he felt led to share that night about dealing with the roots of sin in our lives.

He shared his testimony of being restored from sexual abuse and the Holy Spirit healing him from the experience and breaking him free from a long pornography addiction. He read 1 John 1:7, "But if we walk in the light as He is in the light, we have fellowship with one another, and the blood of Jesus Christ His Son cleanses us from all sin."

I felt the Holy Spirit grip me like fire again, and I knew beyond doubt that I had to publicly confess before the night was over. I determined in my heart to find the right opportunity to speak. As Art wrapped up the teaching on revealing the devil's work and destroying it, the lights came back on in the house, and we saw each other face to face.

The light was turned on. Would we walk in it?

As the group closed I spoke up, "I have a word and a confession."

"Ok," Art said, and leaned forward.

"While I was getting ready to come tonight, the Lord told me that he wanted to perform a cleansing work. I see a connection between what the Lord is doing in the youth group [that the youth leaders work with] and what God is doing here.

"Last week God spoke over each person prophetically. You know that God loves you. Peace has been imparted into the room, and God has provided a presence of peace and love. We started out in the dark, and now we're in the light. I really believe that God is giving us an opportunity tonight to bring things into the light and confess and get free of roots of sin in our lives, and I'd like to start and confess my own sin and then open it up for anyone else to confess and get free.

"I confessed this to Art earlier this week, and I'm embarrassed because I am living this awesome life and Christian adventure that I've always wanted, but still sometimes I fall flat on my face when it comes to lust. And it happens often enough that I know that there's still a hook in my heart keeping me bound. I want to take the opportunity to get free tonight and bring that into the light, and if anyone else wants to, I believe the power is here to set you free."

For the next four hours the group confessed their sins publicly to one another as the Holy Spirit drew things into the light and nailed them to the cross. We cried together as we received freedom from bitterness and un-forgiveness and received healing from wounds and trauma. The Holy Spirit felt like a heavy blanket in the room. He is the Comforter. As sins, wounds, and trauma were healed, physical healing began to occur as well.

Conviction came in waves. Deeper and deeper layers

were exposed in my heart and in others as God's light traveled through our hearts. When the group finally ended, we had been there for eight hours.

The healing experienced by the community was catalyzed and hosted by the prophetic. The Holy Spirit is the Spirit of holiness, and His nature informs all that He does. He is Holy. The Spirit of Holiness who sanctifies, cleanses, revives, and renews is the same Spirit who speaks in words of prophecy, words of knowledge, dreams, visions, discerning of spirits, and the whole prophetic experience.

That evening the Holy Spirit spoke to me, humbled me, convicted me, gripped me, but also empowered me through humility to see freedom. One prophetic word and confession provided the way of freedom for an entire community and instigated a work in the hearts and lives of the fellowship that caused chains to fall off and provided freedom from a whole spectrum of trauma. My small prophecy and confession was one piece of God's work across multiple communities and hundreds of individuals. We were able to be a part of what God was already doing that night.

Our God is an awesome God; He loves His children so much that He paid an incredible price to set them free, and "who the Son sets free is free indeed" (John 8:36). Today Christ is still manifesting Himself to destroy the works of the devil (1 John 3:8). He expresses Himself and speaks through His body, the Church. The voice and Word of God cannot help but cleanse, purify, and make whole. The prophetic is not a pat on the back. It's an invitation to go deeper into the pure and perfect life of Christ.

CONFESSION AND CLEANSING

We have the responsibility to allow God's light to shine on our hearts and His voice to call us into His will and purpose. He speaks with a love that keeps no record of wrongs, but He does not overlook sin. He will not let us destroy ourselves or turn away from growing into who He has called us to be. He loves us enough to speak a Word that demands and empowers living a holy life.

The voice of God evangelizes our hearts day by day. The Holy Spirit speaks to the dark places, healing wounds and reminding us that we are dead to our old lives and new in Christ. He tells us that who we once were is dead—crucified with Christ—and who we are now looks like Jesus. He reveals where we fall short in order to pull us into the fullness of Christ.

The awakening of the conscience and the awareness that we have sinned is the revelation that leads us to repentance. If we don't know or don't believe that we have sinned, we will not turn from that sin; we will live in it. While many believers have an overworked conscience, all of us desperately need the Spirit to shine His light on our lives and show us areas where we must turn to Jesus. We have blind spots in our lives. We have areas where we lack awareness of our own behavior and motivations. We have areas where we have rationalized away the truth that we must change.

The Spirit who prophesies is the same Spirit who reveals sin in order to apply forgiveness and the cleansing power of the blood of Jesus. First John 1:9 states, "If we confess our sins He is faithful and just to forgive us our sins and to cleanse us from all unrighteousness." This does not mean that we must verbally confess every time we sin in order to receive forgiveness. When we came to Christ, we acknowledged our sinful state and our need for a Savior. We now live in a state of forgiveness and relationship with God. We are part of the family. God does not throw us out of the family because we have sinned.

First John 1:9 does mean, however, that we must acknowledge the truth of right and wrong and our need for a Savior. The one who refuses to make a simple acknowledgement that we need forgiveness rejects the forgiveness that God freely offers. But those who hear the voice of God will acknowledge that they have done wrong and receive the forgiveness God offers. Those who hear the prophetic word will step into the light and have their lives cleansed.

> **1 John 1:7 –** But if we walk in the light as He is in the light, we have fellowship with one another, and the blood of Jesus Christ His Son cleanses us from all sin.

Rather than fighting the truth and trying to justify ourselves, we receive the truth that what we did was wrong and the truth that God forgives and cleanses. To reject this truth is to stray from the family and trouble our relationship with God. If we deliberately refuse to repent or to acknowledge sin, we may not be in God's family at all. We may be in the process of leaving God.

In Genesis Three, Adam and Eve hid from the voice of God—their Creator and their Father. In the cool of the evening and at the time and place of intimacy with God, they ran and hid from the voice of Love because they did not want to confess their sin. The distance they tried to put between themselves and God kept them from experiencing His forgiveness and grace until He finally sought them out, establishing the first covenant-promise of a Savior (Genesis 3:15).

In that covenant-promise, today is the day of salvation. Today is the day of cleansing. Today, if we confess our sins, He is faithful and just to forgive us our sins and cleanse us from all unrighteousness (1 John 1:9). We have a promise that God will not treat us as our shame and condemnation tell us we should be treated.

God promises to remove our sin, wipe away the stains, and cleanse us completely. God promises not only to cleanse us of one sin but of all unrighteousness. Our confession of our need for His forgiveness and grace allows Him to wash us completely. This happened on the day we came to Jesus, and God renews this every time we turn to Him and ask. It is not a mechanical system but a relationship of forgiveness and grace. Confusion comes when we stop thinking of God as a Father and try to understand a system of forgiveness apart from a Person. Today, allow the God of love to speak to your heart to convict and to cleanse.

> **2 Corinthians 7:1** – Therefore, having these promises, beloved, let us cleanse ourselves from all filthiness of the flesh and spirit, perfecting holiness in the fear of God.

FORGIVENESS AND THE BODY OF CHRIST

> John 20:21-23 – So Jesus said to them again,
> "Peace to you! As the Father has sent Me, I also
> send you." And when He had said this, He
> breathed on them and said to them, "Receive
> the Holy Spirit. If you forgive the sins of any,
> they are forgiven them; if you retain the sins of
> any, they are retained."

In this passage, Jesus gave the Holy Spirit to the disciples, but He paired the gift of the indwelling Holy Spirit with another gift—the authority to prophetically forgive sins. He gave the disciples the ability to pronounce and enforce the forgiveness of God—to prophesy forgiveness. We are called to proclaim and pronounce forgiveness to the world and to one another. Rarely have I experienced as much life, joy, and freedom as when a brother in the Lord boldly and prophetically proclaims, "In Jesus name, you are forgiven!"

James writes that we should confess our sins to one another that we may be healed (James 5:16). Healing often comes through public confession and public forgiveness because public forgiveness is a prophetic act. It allows the body of Christ to step into the authority and power of Christ by proclaiming His forgiveness and cleansing, and it is the forgiveness and cleansing of Christ that sets the captives free.

God has made a way for community to aid all of us in receiving healing for wounds and freedom from sin. It is by stepping into the light in this way that fellowship is restored with the Father and with one another. And we are cleansed from all sin. (1 John 1:7-9)

Walking in the light should be our daily life. We shouldn't need to confess long lists of sins every day. We should live above deliberate sin, and as we walk in the light and in purity of heart with the Lord, His blood will naturally cleanse us (John 13:10). He continues to wash our feet as we walk along the way of life.

But when we sin deliberately and violate our conscience, obscuring our identity and relationship with the Father, we need to take a big step out of the darkness and into the light. We need to admit that we were wrong and receive forgiveness. We may need to confess our sins to one another to allow others to prophesy forgiveness and cleansing into our lives so that we may be healed.

Today, if there's unconfessed, willful, or deliberate sin in your life, put this book down, find a brother or sister in the Lord who you can trust, confess your sin, and ask him or her to prophesy and proclaim forgiveness and cleansing to you with the authority of Christ. Receive cleansing.

ACTION STEP

Get together with a close friend and read James 5:16. Take a moment to silently listen to the Lord and ask, "Is there any sin in my life I need to confess?"

Relational?
Sexual?
Financial?
Pride?
Integrity?
Dishonesty?
Submission to Authority?
Un-Christlikeness?

Confess to one another. When one confesses, let the other enforce God's grace and forgiveness by saying, "You are forgiven in the name of Jesus." If the Lord does not bring anything to your mind to confess, don't dig something up, and don't pressure others to confess. Simply give the Lord the opportunity to work through confession.

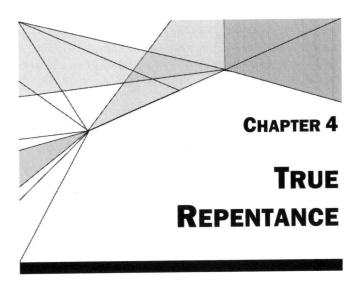

CHAPTER 4

TRUE REPENTANCE

There was a season when I didn't follow any Bible reading plan and simply asked the Lord what I should read each morning. Most of the time, this meant reading whatever I felt like reading, which usually meant reading the epistles. I now spend time reading systematically as well as asking the Lord what I should focus on. One morning I felt the Lord tell me to read James Chapter Four. I turned to it and read:

> **James 4:1-10 –** Where do wars and fights come from among you? Do they not come from your desires for pleasure that war in your members? You lust and do not have. You murder and covet and cannot obtain. You fight and war. Yet you do not have because you do not ask. You ask and do not receive, because you ask amiss, that you may spend it on your pleasures. Adulterers and adulteresses! Do you not know that

friendship with the world is enmity with God? Whoever therefore wants to be a friend of the world makes himself an enemy of God. Or do you think that the Scripture says in vain, "The Spirit who dwells in us yearns jealously"?

But He gives more grace. Therefore He says:

> "God resists the proud,
> But gives grace to the humble."

Therefore submit to God. Resist the devil, and he will flee from you. Draw near to God, and He will draw near to you. Cleanse your hands, you sinners; and purify your hearts, you double-minded. Lament and mourn and weep! Let your laughter be turned to mourning and your joy to gloom. Humble yourselves in the sight of the Lord, and He will lift you up.

I meditated on the passage briefly and thought of a few people in my life it could apply to. I prayed for them and spent some time praying about submitting myself to God and then moved on.

The next morning when I asked God what I should read He said, "James Chapter Four." I turned to the same passage and read it again. I did this for a month. One morning, I turned to James Chapter Four and as I was reading I burst into tears.

It was about me.

The conflict I was having with people came from inside my own heart. It was my fault. The lust I was struggling with came from me. I was the adulterer. These issues came from my lust. I wasn't receiving the things I was asking for from God because I wanted them to glorify myself. I was full of pride. God was resisting me. I needed grace. I was the one sinning. I was the one with the impure heart. I was double minded. It was my time to lament and mourn and weep. I had taken other people's sin seriously, but I had taken my own lightly. It was time to get serious. I humbled myself in the sight of the Lord.

James Chapter Four does not mention the word "repentance," but it describes it. It gives a picture of what repentance often looks and feels like when "godly sorrow" is at work (2 Corinthians 7:10), and it gives step-by-step instructions on how to engage in this form of repentance. I'm still trying to get to the bottom of the depths in these verses, but that moment with God and the repetition of James Chapter Four began a work of God humbling me that is continuing today.

Repentance is our response to God's voice. We choose to think differently after God has spoken. We align our thoughts with His thoughts. We choose to believe differently after God has spoken. We set our faith on His sure promise. We choose to act differently. We obey His voice. Turning toward the voice of God results in transformation. He is calling us to Him and deeper into who we are in Him.

It is popular to believe that repentance is simply a change of mind—that it is a renewal in our thinking. It is that, but it is so much more as any Greek and Hebrew dictionary reveals. Many current Bible teachers pick tiny excerpts from these definitions to prove what they want, rather than citing the full meaning of the word. Repentance is a change of mind, heart, and action. It is a turning away from sin and a turning toward God. It is both a submission to God and a resistance of the devil.

Jesus announced repentance before the Holy Spirit was able to renew people's minds (Matthew 3:2). He commanded repentance because of the presence of God's Kingdom and the arrival of His own ministry as King of God's Kingdom. His command to repent means to submit to the rule and reign of God in the here and now.

John the Baptist warned his hearers to change their actions when they repented. He told them not to hold onto some intellectual or theological idea that would make them feel secure and protected regardless of persisting in sin. He said, "Therefore bear fruits worthy of repentance, and do not begin to say to yourselves, 'We have Abraham as our father.' For I say to you that God is able to raise up children to Abraham from these stones" (Luke 3:8).

Some of the Pharisees took pride in their pedigrees as Jews and as children of Abraham. They believed their identity as children of Abraham meant that they were righteous. John the Baptist warned them that if their actions did not demonstrate their faith, they were in danger.

In the same way, our actions demonstrate our hearts. A famous Bible teacher said, "Your life lived is your heart revealed." God knows both your heart and your life. He commands repentance that goes beyond how you think to your whole way of being.

John the Baptist followed this admonishment with practical instruction on what repentance meant for people in various ways and walks of life.

Luke 3:10-14 – So the people asked him, saying, "What shall we do then?"

> He answered and said to them, "He who
> has two tunics, let him give to him who has
> none; and he who has food, let him do
> likewise."
>
> Then tax collectors also came to be
> baptized, and said to him, "Teacher, what shall
> we do?"
>
> And he said to them, "Collect no more than
> what is appointed for you."
>
> Likewise the soldiers asked him, saying,
> "And what shall we do?"
>
> So he said to them, "Do not intimidate
> anyone or accuse falsely, and be content with
> your wages."

In each case John taught them to turn away from selfish and sinful behavior and turn toward the goodness of God. The greedy were to give in generosity. The dishonest were to be honest. The bullies were to handle their authority and power well. This was a change in lifestyle, in behavior, and in action; but it was not mere behavior modification. They wanted to change. God's voice was not only a command, but an invitation. The wonder of God's expressed word is that it has the power to create a desire for His will. They desired to repent and asked how. John gave them practical instructions of what to do. The fulfillment of those instructions would demonstrate a changed heart.

This is not merely an Old-Covenant teaching. New Covenant preaching demonstrated the same emphasis on turning not only in mind and heart, but in behavior and action:

> **Acts 26:20 –** ...but declared first to those in Damascus and in Jerusalem, and throughout all the region of Judea, and then to the Gentiles, that they should repent, turn to God, and do works befitting repentance.

Sometimes repenting meant restitution. This always meant overcoming evil with good. Licentiousness was to be replaced with purity, greed with generosity, hate with love and kindness.

Repentance is more than confession of sin. We must confess our sin and acknowledge that our sin is in fact sinful in order to repent, but confession itself is not repentance.

I continued playing cash poker games after I was saved. I gambled large sums of money and even intentionally manipulated people into losing their money to me. I did not believe this was wrong and even prayed for God's help before games. Until I realized and confessed that it was wrong, I could not repent. Once I confessed that this was sin, I repented and only played poker again for small change as a pass-time. Repentance meant that I stopped that behavior.

Repentance is a change of heart, but it does not always require emotional upheaval. I used to think that if I felt enough guilt, or shame, or "conviction," I would really change. This is not true. We can't earn repentance with tears. Tears are often a part of true repentance and confession, but they do not effect change. Life-changing repentance can be calm and quiet or loud and emotional.

It is not wrong to lament. Jesus said, "Woe to you, Chorazin! Woe to you, Bethsaida! For if the mighty works which were done in you had been done in Tyre and Sidon, they would have repented long ago in sackcloth and ashes" (Matthew 11:21). He implies that mourning would have been the appropriate response.

God wants us to know and believe the truth and have our emotions align with that truth. Unfortunately our emotions often respond to lies. This most obviously appears in depressed and defeated Christians, but a more subtle form occurs in believers who live in sin yet feel immense pride.

Jesus warned these cities that their irresponsiveness to God's love and grace and the magnitude of their sin should have provoked mourning. Instead, they were numb. They rejected Jesus and the truth. Today Jesus is tuning our hearts to respond to His voice.

James told the sinful church that they should mourn. He told them that they needed to align their hearts with the truth. They needed to confess the horrific sinful state they were living in and let it break their hearts. They were continuing in pride and using joy as a sham to keep themselves from the truth of their sin. They were putting on a happy face. They were pretending that they were OK. They were sleeping with people who were not their spouses and then going to church and getting their praise on. James was telling them that God would rather have them break down in tears and genuinely repent of their sin than to come and offer empty praise.

James told them to cleanse their hands. This means they were to stop whatever sin they were engaged in. They were to let go of whatever sin they were holding onto. They were to open their hands, drop their sin, and let the blood of Jesus cleanse them.

He told them to purify their hearts. They were to let

God touch their desires and let His Spirit change them. They were to renounce lust, hatred, and greed. They were to embrace purity, love, and generosity. Their grief was meant to humble them. Things were not OK. They needed to stop pretending and allow themselves to go to God and say, "I'm really messed up, and I need Your help." And they needed to really mean it. Saying that with genuine emotion often means a cry of mourning.

REPENTANCE DOES NOT MEAN FREEDOM FROM TEMPTATION

We will always be tempted in different ways. As we grow, certain temptations will fade, and we will become stronger. As we resist the devil, he will consistently flee. However, the devil tempted Jesus and never gave up even after Jesus resisted him perfectly. The Bible says, "Now when the devil had ended every temptation, he departed from Him until an opportune time" (Luke 4:13).

If Jesus was tempted for His entire life on earth, even after perfect resistance, you will be also. I used to try to have experiences with God that would somehow instantly sanctify me and end temptation in my life. This will never happen. We will have to resist the devil, and we can.

James commands us to submit to God first—the first step to repentance. We must give our lives to Christ as King. We must submit to God as master over us. Romans 12:1-2 does not mention the word "repentance" but describes this transformation:

> **Romans 12:1-2 –** I beseech you therefore, brethren, by the mercies of God, that you

present your bodies a living sacrifice, holy,
acceptable to God, which is your reasonable
service. And do not be conformed to this world,
but be transformed by the renewing of your
mind, that you may prove what is that good and
acceptable and perfect will of God.

Paul urged His readers to present their bodies, their
vessels, their instruments of action, to God as living
sacrifices. This means that we are available to God for life
or death or any action or obedience in any way at any time.
This is our worship and reasonable service. *Here is my body.
Here is my vessel. You can use it to go wherever You want, God.
You can use it to do whatever You want, God. I will only use it for
Your good pleasure in my life.*

Paul went on to instruct the Roman church not to
be conformed to this world. Our past, our history, and the
whole world around us teach us lies. They tell us to rebel
against God, to believe false teaching, and to reject the
truth of God. We must be transformed by allowing God's
voice to change the way we think so that we can know and
do the will of God.

The first step is to truly give ourselves to God as
living sacrifices—to put ourselves on the altar and to crawl
back on that altar every time we slip off. We must confess
our sins and receive God's forgiveness. We must be honest
with ourselves about the truth of our condition. We must
submit to God and then resist the devil's temptation. God
will not resist the enemy for us. We must hear God's
voice, acknowledge God's truth, and say "no" to sin.

I wish this process was always easy, but it's often
not. Repentance is an act of faith, not of works. It is also
both a crisis and a process. Repentance must be walked

out day by day. I've found instant repentance in many areas of life. There are times when I have repented and never struggled with that sin again. I repented of manipulating people out of their money at poker and never did it again. I'm virtually never tempted to do it again, either. I am walking out repentance in this area.

Many other areas of life are a daily submission to God and resistance of the devil. Some remained areas of regular failure for years. In some cases, I sought repentance for years without truly finding it. I would confess over and over. I would be free for some time and then fall back again. I would cry out to God again and again, but I struggled to truly submit to God and to truly resist the devil. I let sin have its way and gave in to temptation regularly. I needed help to find true repentance.

We repent by faith. Repentance is our responsibility, but only God can change our hearts. We place our hearts before Him and trust Him to change them. We confess our sins, and we turn by His grace. Our hearts can deceive us. We can continue on in lies and false repentance. We can confess without truly repenting. We can hold onto sin in the back of our minds and the dark corners of our hearts. But the Holy Spirit never relents. He speaks truth and love. He will call us back to the altar and give us the strength to lay down our lives to the One who truly loves us.

God truly loves you. He empowers you to change. As I learned later, God will do whatever it takes to free us and give us genuine repentance if we are willing to receive it.

2 Timothy 2:25 states that repentance is something God gives:

2 Timothy 2:25 – … in humility correcting those who are in opposition, if God perhaps will grant them repentance, so that they may know the truth.

Repentance is also a grace of God. God grants repentance and gives it to each one of us. He overcomes the stubborn rebellion of our hearts. He calls us and draws us and penetrates every area of our hearts with the gospel (Acts 5:31).

The altar is prepared for you today. If you have confessed but not truly repented of your sin, lay yourself on the altar, renounce lies and sin, give your body to God today as His living sacrifice. Let Him touch and change your heart, your mind, and your life forever.

ACTION STEP

Is the Holy Spirit bringing anything to your mind that you must turn away from? Verbally pray out repentance of any of these issues in your life. Even if you don't feel conviction in these areas, I encourage you to search your heart and verbally pray aloud, renouncing and turning from sin.

Lord, I confess that I have participated in _____. Thank You for Your forgiveness. I renounce and repent of any and all involvement in _____. I will never do that again. I turn away from that, and I turn to You, Father. In Jesus' name, Amen.

Idolatry

Lord, I confess that I have had _____ as an idol in my life. Thank You for Your forgiveness. I renounce and repent of any and all idolatry regarding _____. I worship You alone. I ask You to help me keep _____ in its proper place. I will never worship an idol again. I turn away from that, and I turn to You, Father. In Jesus' name, Amen.

Fear

Lord, I confess that I have feared _____. I renounce the fear of _____, and I cancel out any and all ground the enemy has gained in my life through this activity. You have not given me a spirit of fear. I choose to walk by faith in You and Your promise to protect and provide. In Jesus' name, Amen.

Rebellion

Lord, I confess that I have been rebellious toward _____ by [name the specific ways]. Thank You for forgiving me. I choose to be submissive and obedient to You and Your Word and to anyone You tell me to. In Jesus' name, Amen.

Pride

Lord, I confess that I have been proud in _____. Thank You for forgiving me. I choose to humble myself before You and others. In Jesus' name, Amen.

Bondages (Sinful Habits and Addictions)

Lord, I confess that I have committed the sin of _____. Thank You for forgiving me and cleansing me. I turn from this sin and turn to You, Lord. Break all bondage, all chains, and anything binding me to this sin. I will never do that again. I turn away from that, and I turn to You, Father. In Jesus' name, Amen.

Sexual Immorality

Lord, I renounce _____ with [name any person involved]. Thank You for forgiving me and cleansing me. I turn from this sin and turn to You, Lord. I ask You to break any wrong or sinful bond with [name of other person involved]. I renounce all these uses of my body as an instrument of unrighteousness. I will never do that again. I turn away from that, and I turn to You, Father. I choose to present my body to You as an instrument of righteousness—pure and holy in Your sight, by Your blood. I present my body as a living sacrifice to You. I reject the lie that I am dirty, unclean, or sinful. In Jesus' name, Amen.

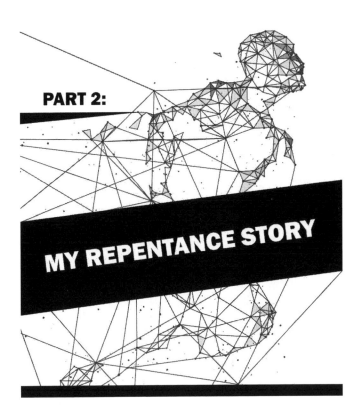

PART 2:

MY REPENTANCE STORY

The Church is full of people who struggle daily to change. They know they need to change. They want to change. They want to repent of sin. But they struggle on without finding lasting repentance.

I am touched by this struggle. Their story was my story. I remember the frustration and hopelessness of addiction. I remember desperately longing for change and for repentance. I remember reading book after book and begging God for freedom.

God answered my prayer. What follows is the story of how God's voice called me out of pornography addiction. Surveys demonstrate that pornography is a regular struggle for the majority of Christian ministers, as well as the majority of the Christian church.

The specifics of my story will be relevant for many readers. But even if this is not your personal struggle, the principles of repentance in God's Word are relevant for all. Some parts of my story are challenging, but I have joy and freedom because of what God has done in my life. My desire is that this testimony and teaching brings you into that joy and freedom, no matter what your present struggle may be.

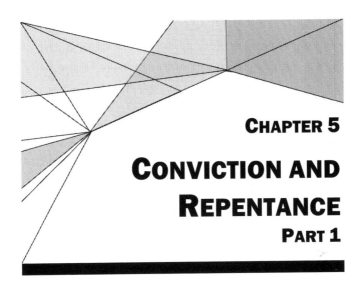

CHAPTER 5

CONVICTION AND REPENTANCE
PART 1

I had been addicted to pornography since before I was saved; and while that addiction loosened when I came to the Lord, it continued off and on into my Christian walk. I fell into a painful cycle of confessing sin, repenting, and falling back into deliberate lust and pornography. I had read books on the subject, confessed to multiple people—often again and again, sometimes even daily—and I'd gone through an internet course with an online accountability partner. Nothing brought lasting freedom.

When God called me to enter full-time missions work in Detroit, I found a long period of freedom and the ability to leave all addiction behind. Unfortunately, I found out that ministry was not what I had imagined. The leader who began mentoring me was in the middle of a mental and emotional breakdown and a number of moral failures that eventually caused him to lose his credentials and ordination. The stress of the situation and the unresolved wounds and issues in my own heart caused me to fall back into pornography less than a year into full-time ministry.

I hated addiction. Along with the destructive and toxic ministry environment came depression and anxiety. I found myself barely able to function. I sought help from the Lord and spent many hours crying out for help and weeping before God. I hated my life.

While I was in Detroit, a powerful move of God broke out in the church I had attended in Pennsylvania. A fiery and anointed evangelist led a two-week revival that resulted in numerous decisions for the Lord, miraculous healings, and a shaking in the church. I was far away at the time and heard testimonies from my family, but it caused more heartache than joy as the hope I had for revival in my own life became more deferred. "Hope deferred makes the heart sick" (Proverbs 13:12). My heart was sick.

The unhealthy ministry leader I mentioned was removed by his denomination, and the ministry began to receive restoration for the things that had occurred. I began to grow healthier and experience more of the Holy Spirit's work.

My family told me that the evangelist whose ministry had so transformed their church was returning for more meetings. I determined not to miss out on the power of God. I had experienced much more in the prophetic at this point as well as God's healing power, and I was eager to find the power of God for my generation even though I was not free myself. I was conflicted and doubleminded. I would spend days in prayer and fasting but then fall into pornography and depression days later.

Before the evangelist started the meetings, I had worked through ministry materials on repentance, and I had been free three weeks. I wanted to be free and hoped the Evangelist would call me out and lay hands on me. I wanted the power of God, but pride still had a hold on my heart. As I've gone on to minister to those struggling with addictions of many different kinds, I've learned that pride is inevitably intertwined in addictive behavior. Genuine honesty about addiction is emotionally difficult, and pride allows lies to cover that pain.

The trip from Detroit to Pennsylvania was difficult. I was eagerly looking forward to the meetings, but I was finding it hard to pray. Conviction was starting to seep in past my confidence. After three weeks without looking at pornography I thought I was surely free.

The first evening meeting I sat in after an hour-long drive, my brother introduced me to the Evangelist before the service. He was an intimidating man. I hoped he would call me out, prophesy to me, and impart power for me to minister. During the service the presence of God was thick, and I loved it. The atmosphere was full of joy and fire. The Evangelist preached a simple message on healing, but before he prayed for the sick he ordered everyone to close their eyes and bow their heads:

"Not everybody within the sound of my voice is right with God." A sudden powerful fire lit in my spirit nearly making me weep and double over. It was one of the most intense feelings I've ever had and certainly the most intense conviction I've ever experienced.

This must be condemnation, I thought, *It's been three weeks since I watched pornography.* I began to whisper under my breath, "Jesus you know I love you. You know I love you. You know I love you."

The evangelist continued, "You know, loving God. . . There are people that will be in hell that love Jesus and love God, but they never lived holy. They didn't love Him enough to receive Him and push sin out of their life, and say, 'God if you told me to live holy, then I'm going to live holy. I'm not going to look at pornography.'"

A fire of fear surged within my heart.

He continued, "'I'm not going to drink intoxicating liquors. I'm not going to do drugs. I'm not going to do what you called me out of. I'm not going to go to wild parties on Fridays and Saturdays. I'm yours, I'm going to live as a child of God.' See, I have meetings like this all year long, every year, and I see people—they love the anointing, in fact if I were to give an altar call right now, you'd want hands laid on you. And I will lay hands on you. But first things first: You need to get right with God. Because if you were honest with me and honest with God, there is sin in your life. There are things that you've made a part of your lifestyle that will keep you out of heaven."

I knew he was talking about me. I was the one who loved the anointing. I was the one who wanted hands laid on me. I was the one who needed to get right with God. But I was terribly confused. I had repented over and over again. I thought I was forgiven.

"You have to make up your mind to be a clean, pure, holy vessel that God can use—to repent of sin, to come out of wickedness, and come into the light of God," he added, "Tonight's your night. If you're here tonight, and you're not living exactly as you should for God— there's sin in your life that you need to get rid of, and you say, 'tonight's my night, I'm coming into God, never to go out again. I'm going to live for Jesus Christ. I want Him in my heart. I want His power in me, and I'll never go back'—if that's you tonight, I want to see your hand up high in Jesus' name."

I felt fire on my hand and arm, but I couldn't do it. The people in this church knew me. My family was in the pew beside me. These people knew I was a missionary. I didn't understand. I saw people healed in my ministry. I had dreams and visions. I had prophesied. How could this be true?

A few people responded to the altar call.

"There's more. . . There's more!" he pressed, "Why are you going to sit in the anointing and feel that presence of God—knowing full well you're not living right—and turn your back and go out those double doors knowing your name's not written in the Lamb's book of life?"

A chorus of screams was coming from inside me. I was born again. Jesus had come into my heart. How could my name not be written in the Lamb's book of life? But the fire would not leave. It squeezed tighter and tighter on the inside.

But I refused to raise my hand. I couldn't.

"If you sleep with women that aren't your wife, you'll go to hell. If you sleep with men that aren't your husband—if you have sex with people you're not married to—you'll go to hell. God said that; that's not my opinion. He said the sexually immoral will not enter the kingdom of heaven."

God! I screamed inside, *It's been three weeks!*

"If you were going to sit before God and watch the last four weeks of your life, just you and God in a private screening, you're ready to do that? Or is their sin in your life you need to get rid of? If you need to get rid of sin, I want to see your hand. Before we go any further, I want to see your hand."

How did he know? How did he know four weeks was the right number? I was terrified and confused. I had been so sure I was right with God.

A few more responded to the altar call.

"Be honest with yourself. Be honest with God! Make tonight the night you get saved. Anyone else anywhere, I'll wait ten more seconds. God's wrestling with your heart; give in to Him. Five seconds. Anyone else, anywhere."

A few more raised their hands.

"Quickly. I want everyone who lifted a hand to come to this altar in Jesus's name. . ."

The altar call was over, but the hand of fire still squeezed deep inside. I could barely function. I mumbled something to my friends and family and drove back to a hotel with my friend. I confessed everything to him and then collapsed on my face into the carpet. I wept on the floor and repented for hours. I could not shake the fear and fire on my heart. I went to sleep that night still crying and repenting. My heart was broken—torn in pieces.

As soon as I woke up the next day, I got on my face before the Lord and began to weep and pray again. Hours more went by. My friend tried to console me, "You've brought your sin into the light," he said. "It's over. Its power is broken."

But I couldn't shake the conviction.

I wept and prayed until lunchtime when we had plans to eat with my family. I was quiet the whole meal. We went down and sat in the Evangelist's afternoon teaching meeting. I was still numb with fear. When we went back to the hotel, I wept and prayed some more as my friend counseled me.

That night we went to the evening meeting. The Evangelist gave an altar call for those in bondage and in need of deliverance from sin and oppression. I responded. The tangible fear of the Lord did not leave me until weeks later, and even now as I write this, I tremble.

But I was finally free.

Our experiences with the Holy Spirit working through the body of Christ don't always fit into theological boxes. Many may question if I had lost my salvation or perhaps even if I was genuinely saved previous to this experience. I know that I was genuinely born again of the Spirit of God. But I also know that I was backslidden. Few would have known, and no one but the Holy Spirit would have told me I was backslidden. But God had identified something in me.

I witnessed to the lost almost every day. I spent hours in prayer. I read ten or more chapters of the Bible every day. But I was double-minded. I found myself trapped in a never-ending cycle of confession of sin, forgiveness, and failure.

It is not holiness that saves us. The thief on the cross beside Jesus had no time to be sanctified. It is faith that saves us. But sin and ungodliness shipwreck our faith. Somewhere along the way, sin had poisoned my heart and my life. I was losing faith. The saving grace of my life was that during times of repentance I cried out to God and said, "Whatever it takes, Lord, to be free, I'll do it. I'll do whatever it takes."

God answered my request.

It took a life-altering experience with the power of the Holy Spirit and the voice of the Lord to break me free. My sin was identified by a "word of knowledge," and I was prophetically called to account. I was not allowed to believe that God would tolerate my sin. The voice of God called me to holiness.

Almost every time I tell this story, people suggest that perhaps the Evangelist ministered in the wrong spirit, but I have no doubt that he did exactly as the Lord told him. I have since met and spoken with him many times. He remains the most powerful preacher I have ever known, one of the greatest benefits to my own ministry, and one of the greatest examples of what power is available in the life of a servant of God. I believe this instance was unquestionably God dealing with the sin in my heart, and it bore fruit.

I am grateful that God called out my sin prophetically and did not allow me to continue in it. As difficult, terrifying, and shattering as the experience was, it has drawn me into the arms of God. I was in a place where the love of God was no longer motivating me to holiness, and Jesus gave me a taste of the fear of God, which made me run back into the arms of a loving Father.

I have the audio of that service, and I still tremble when I listen to it. God requires a holy life. He does not compromise. Righteousness is not some invisible, ephemeral, spiritual thing without substance or reality. It's practical, and it's real.

Practical righteousness is a holy life. A holy life is the evidence of a faith that receives the righteousness of Christ.

If you are not living in holiness and above willful sin, you are living in a dangerous place. The end of sin is death and destruction.

John 3:16 – God loved the world so much that He gave His one and only Son that whoever believes in Him should not die but have everlasting life.

There is no place for deliberate, willful sin in the life of the believer. I don't mean sinful attitudes or sinful thoughts. I'm not talking about emotional outbursts or sudden mistakes. I'm not talking about blind spots or even bad habits. I am talking about situations where we know what is right, we know what is wrong, and we deliberately and consciously choose to sin because we want to. Deep in our hearts, we know that we will be forgiven later. We presume on God's grace and forgiveness.

Believers can and must live above conscious, deliberate, willful sin.

Hebrews 10:26-27 – For if we sin willfully after we have received the knowledge of the truth, there no longer remains a sacrifice for sins, but a certain fearful expectation of judgment and fiery indignation, which will devour the adversaries.

Those who live a lifestyle of deliberate, willful sin are rejecting Christ in their actions and will suffer eternity in hell. Hebrews goes on to describe that Esau sought repentance over and over again with tears but could never find it. He wanted to change what he had done and what he was doing. He couldn't find repentance. That is not you. You live in grace. You live in the empowerment of the Spirit. You live in the love of the Father and the covenant of redemption. You can turn back today.

It is impossible to know who has stepped over that line or when that line has been crossed. Many struggle sincerely with addictions, habits, and patterns of sin but sincerely repent and continue to walk in faith. But those who continually make a conscious, premeditated decision to sin are not safe.

The evidence of true repentance is that you stop sinning. John the Baptist instructed all to bear fruits that demonstrate true repentance (Matthew 3:8). In other words, let your life show that you have truly changed and turned away from sin. Jesus said, "Go and sin no more," not, "Go and sin less." (John 8:10).

Sin is falling short of Jesus Christ, and anything that is not of faith is sin (Romans 14:23). We all fall short of Jesus in many ways. As James writes, "For we all stumble in many things" (James 3:2a). I am not talking about Christian "perfection;" I am talking about Christian "purity."

It is possible for Christians to have a pure heart—to walk with a sincere singleness of purpose. We may make mistakes. We may stumble. We may even fall. But our hearts remain in the hands of Christ. We turn from our sin and get back up. Genuine faith causes us to rise and shake off failure to walk in true holiness and the love of the Lord.

> **Proverbs 24:16** – For a righteous man may fall seven times and rise again, but the wicked shall fall by calamity.

These principles are developed further in the next chapter, but if you are being convicted or struggling with addiction now, know that God's grace is available to free you immediately. You don't have to experience what I did. Few people experience freedom that way. Most find freedom in their daily walk with Jesus and grow in freedom as they experience more of the Holy Spirit. Many are freed through a moment of genuine honesty with God and simple repentance. Let the Holy Spirit speak to you and shine His light on your heart.

Are you being honest with God? Are you being honest with yourself? Have you really repented of your sin? Or, deep down, do you intend to do it again? Are you presuming on God's forgiveness? Ask the Lord these questions. Don't torment yourself with them. God answers prayer, and He will either give you assurance or the gift of repentance (Romans 8:16; 2 Timothy 2:25).

ACTION STEP

Ask God:

➤ Father, have I been honest with You and with myself about repentance? Lord, am I holding on to any sin in my heart?

➤ Deep down have I believed that I can sin and get away with it? Have I believed that sin won't affect my heart?

➤ Deep down have I believed that unrighteous people will still go to Heaven?

Allow God to deal with you on these issues. Confess and renounce false beliefs if you need to. End your time by worshipping God in the assurance that His grace changes hearts and minds.

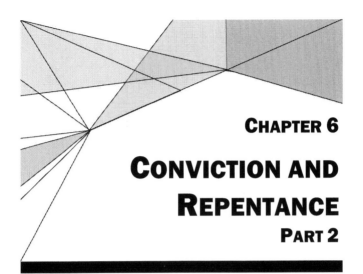

CHAPTER 6

CONVICTION AND REPENTANCE
PART 2

I remember one summer when I was home from college I gave in to temptation and watched pornography. I felt no conviction. I had worn my conscience out. I avoided thinking about sin. I sat and watched shows on my computer for three days straight. I refused to think about God, Jesus, sin, conviction, or anything. I turned myself off. The third morning I woke up shouting from my sleep, "Jesus help me!" at the top of my lungs. I rolled out of bed and collapsed onto my knees in tears. I could not keep running from God. I could not live without Him.

"But if we walk in the light as He is in the light, we have fellowship with one another and the blood of Jesus Christ cleanses us from all sin" (1 John 1:7). Purity means walking in the light, acknowledging our faults, confessing our sins, and repenting when we need to change direction.

Many times we do not need to confess or even repent. Our lives are on the right path, and our hearts are pointed in the right direction. Maybe we said an unkind word that we immediately regretted, or indulged in a

thought we shouldn't have, but we turned away from it
almost without thinking. In times like these our presence
in the light and in relationship with Christ means that we
receive an almost unconscious cleansing. Jesus washes our
feet (John 13:10). It is our feet that get dirty as we walk
around in this fallen world. The rest of us remains clean
because we have been washed in the blood of Christ,
cleansed of all sin.

> **1 John 5:16-17 –** If anyone sees his brother
> sinning a sin which does not lead to death, he
> will ask, and He will give him life for those who
> commit sin not leading to death. There is sin
> leading to death. I do not say that he should
> pray about that. All unrighteousness is sin, and
> there is sin not leading to death.

John made a distinction between sins—those
leading to death and those not leading to death. It is less
than Jesus to say an unkind word or to curse when we
injure ourselves. Jesus would not do that. It is a sin not to
reach the lost. It is a sin not to make disciples. Yet these
are often not deliberate acts of disobedience. They are less
than Jesus, and we must repent, but they are not a willful
breaking of fellowship with Christ. Deliberate sin does
break relationship with Christ; and if we continue, that sin
will lead to death.

John said that we should pray for each other when
we see areas in our brothers and sisters lives that reveal
that we are living less than Jesus. We need to be watchful
over our lives and the lives of those around us for sins that
do not lead to death because they are evidence that our
guard is down and that we may be drifting into more

serious sin. However, John did not instruct us to pray for those who are living in willful, disobedient sin—not because they are hopeless or because prayer is wrong, but because they need the Word to bring them to repentance. They need to hear the voice of God.

David prayed, "Keep back your servant also from presumptuous sins; let them not have dominion over me! Then I shall be blameless and innocent of great transgression" (Psalm 19:13). Abstaining from all known sin means we are walking in innocence, not perfection. We are keeping our conscience and walking rightly before the Lord in the light that we have. The Holy Spirit will continue to reveal sinful attitudes and mature us in our internal lives. That work will continue until we reach the fullness of Christ.

> **Galatians 5:19-21 –** Now the works of the flesh are evident, which are: adultery, fornication, uncleanness, lewdness, idolatry, sorcery, hatred, contentions, jealousies, outbursts of wrath, selfish ambitions, dissensions, heresies, envy, murders, drunkenness, revelries, and the like; of which I tell you beforehand, just as I also told you in time past, that those who practice such things will not inherit the kingdom of God.

Paul was clear that these sins lead to death. They violate our identity in Christ and forsake our role as heirs and inheritors of salvation in the kingdom of God. We should read over this list soberly. Paul wrote to the Galatians that these sinful activities are "evident," meaning obviously wrong. He also wrote that these sins would keep us from the kingdom. He wrote "just as I told you in time past." Paul had preached this to the Galatians before. It was part of his message and part of his doctrine that these deliberate willful acts of sin violate salvation. Paul corroborated this doctrine in 1 Corinthians:

> **1 Corinthians 6:9-10 –** Do you not know that the unrighteous will not inherit the kingdom of God? Do not be deceived. Neither fornicators, nor idolaters, nor adulterers, nor homosexuals, nor sodomites, nor thieves, nor covetous, nor drunkards, nor revilers, nor extortioners will inherit the kingdom of God.

Paul qualified those who practice these behaviors as "the unrighteous." We are only righteous by faith in Christ—not by our works or even by our holiness. Justification and righteousness are obtained and walked out by faith, and practical holiness is the evidence of this faith. This list in 1 Corinthians 6:9-10, however, is a list of identities. These men and women lived out these sins to the point where their behavior became the identifying aspect of their lives rather than their faith in the gospel. They proved their faith invalid. They lost faith.

Paul then reminded the wayward Corinthians of their true identity and the work of Christ.

> **1 Corinthians 6:11 –** And such were some of you. But you were washed, but you were sanctified, but you were justified in the name of the Lord Jesus and by the Spirit of our God.

This was prophetic. He reminded them of their testimony. He reminded them of their identity in Christ.

He reminded them of what God had done, and he told them how God saw them: washed, sanctified, justified. This identity is powerful. It is this identity in Christ that is the fountainhead of holiness. The voice of God is the only way we can truly know who we are, and only by knowing and seeing our identity in Him—by gazing into that mirror of revelation—can we live a holy life.

We must cling to what Christ has done and who Christ has made us. We must not forget what we look like in the Spirit. We must not violate our identity or violate our faith. John's revelation of Jesus contains the harrowing reminder:

> **Revelation 21:8 –** But the cowardly, unbelieving, abominable, murderers, sexually immoral, sorcerers, idolaters, and all liars shall have their part in the lake which burns with fire and brimstone, which is the second death.

These are not far-off sins. We must be both humble and vigilant. Paul the apostle, who is esteemed as perhaps the greatest man in the history of the world next to Jesus, wrote,

> **1 Corinthians 9:27 –** But I discipline my body and bring it into subjection, lest, when I have preached to others, I myself should become disqualified.

In other words, even with all of his accomplishments, all of his service, all of his miracles—the raising of the dead, the healing of the sick, the third-heaven revelations, and the boldness that endured incomparable persecution—he still needed to watch over his life and rule his body so that he would not be among those who fell away from the faith, disqualified for the kingdom. An old saying declares, "God is the only employer who will fire you and let you keep working for Him." The history of the restoration of the prophetic in the twentieth century is riddled with heroes of the gift who fell into immorality. Paul fought to not become such a person.

God still calls us out of sin. He may call us in love and gentleness. If our hearts have grown cold, if we have grown lukewarm, or if we have left our first love, He may call us in the fear of the Lord. Still, it is the sweet voice of the Savior.

> **1 John 3:6 –** Whoever abides in Him does not sin. Whoever sins has neither seen Him nor known Him.

Abiding and remaining in relationship with Jesus keeps us from sin. When we walk and talk with Jesus—when we respond to the voice of God that keeps us in the light and free from sin—He gives us real freedom. How do we abide in this relationship with God? By the prophetic revelation of the Spirit:

> **1 John 2:27 –** But the anointing which have received from Him abides in you and you do not need that anyone teach you; but as the same anointing teaches you concerning all things, and is true, and is not a lie, and just as it has taught you, you will abide in Him.

We abide with Jesus, we remain with Jesus, we walk with Jesus, and we are hidden in Jesus by the Holy Spirit who never leaves us and teaches and reveals all things to us. The Spirit leads us in the truth, and as He teaches us and gives us revelation—as He speaks to us—we remain and abide and rest in relationship with the King of kings and the Lord of lords.

As the Spirit teaches us and leads us into all truth, He convicts us of sin, righteousness, and judgment (John 16:8). He convicts, but He does not condemn. Conviction is Good News because it reveals that God has a solution. God has a cleansing. God has an answer for our sin, and God is speaking to us. Conviction over sin is the revelation of the Holy Spirit saying, "That was wrong; that is not who you are; I have something better for you; this is what righteousness looks like; this is what's missing from your walk." Conviction is evidence of a pure heart. Conviction is evidence that we're still in fellowship with the Lord because we are still hearing His voice. We are being pulled back into right relationship with Him.

Conviction and condemnation are often confused. Conviction comes from the Holy Spirit. Condemnation comes from the devil. Conviction leads you out of sin. Condemnation accuses you of remaining in sin. Conviction identifies the specific sin that must change. Condemnation accuses your whole person. Conviction deals with present sin. Condemnation speaks of the past of what has gone behind you. Conviction makes you holy. Condemnation makes you weak. Conviction strengthens you to change. Condemnation says you can't change. Conviction says you're guilty of sin and restores you. Condemnation says you're guilty of sin, and you will be punished. Conviction says there's hope to change. Condemnation says hope is lost.

The confusion often comes because both conviction and condemnation can cause sorrow. When we experience sorrow over sin, the source could be either conviction or condemnation. It is popular to believe that there should be no sorrow in the Christian experience or that sorrow is not part of God's work, but Paul clarified that godly sorrow comes from the conviction of the Holy Spirit and produces good fruit in our lives:

> **2 Corinthians 7:10-11 –** For godly sorrow produces repentance leading to salvation, not to be regretted; but the sorrow of the world produces death. For observe this very thing, that you sorrowed in a godly manner: What diligence it produced in you, what clearing of yourselves, what indignation, what fear, what vehement desire, what zeal, what vindication! In all these things you proved yourselves to be clear in this matter.

Godly sorrow produces repentance, a change of directions, and because it produces repentance, it should never be regretted. I do not regret the hours I spent on the carpet, or having my sin identified by a word of knowledge, or having to humble myself in public confession. Though it was painful, it set me free. Part of me still grieves that Jesus had to deal with me that way and that I was in such danger, but I'm writing this in hope that the godly sorrow that I experienced will spare those who read this from similar sorrow.

Paul wrote that godly sorrow should produce:

> Diligence
> Clearing of yourselves (of guilt, of sin, of accusation)
> Indignation
> Fear
> Vehement desire
> Zeal
> Vindication

All of these things are positive and to be desired. But condemnation often paralyzes us from action. If it doesn't produce healthy action, it's usually self-abuse.

Conviction produces action. It produces repentance. It produces a diligent exposure of sin and a diligent walk in discipline as we clear ourselves of sin, guilt, and accusation. It produces indignation in us against sin, so the next time the devil comes to tempt us we become indignant at the suggestion of entering something that produced such destruction in our lives. Godly sorrow produces the fear of the Lord; we begin to love what He loves and hate what He hates. It produces a vehement desire for holiness, and we begin to pursue Jesus, the kingdom, and His righteousness. It produces zeal for Him and vindicates us in a walk of holiness.

Conviction is the voice of God. Condemnation is the voice of the devil. But in the middle of this confrontation is our own heart and conscience. There is no condemnation in Christ (Romans 8:1), yet John turned the tables and wrote,

1 John 3:20-21 – For if our heart condemns us, God is greater than our heart, and knows all

things. Beloved if our heart does not condemn
us, we have confidence toward God.

We were never meant to experience condemnation
in our hearts. The primary weapon and freedom from
condemnation is living a holy life. If we live holy, above
deliberate, conscious sin, condemnation will have no hold
on us. If we live in the middle, we will always have to sort
out which is which. We will always be wrestling with the
voice of the enemy because he knows he has the grounds
to lie to us. If we walk in holiness, we walk in the truth,
and every lie will fall at our feet.

If we walk out a lie, our heart will condemn us. It
will tell us that we are worthy of judgment. What is your
heart telling you now?

1 John 2:1-2 – My little children these things I
write to you, so that you may not sin. And if
anyone sins, we have an Advocate with the
Father, Jesus Christ the righteous. And He
Himself is the propitiation for our sins, and not
for ours only but also for the whole world.

Jesus died for our sins. He took them on Himself.
He became sin, so we could become the righteousness of
God. He stands as our Advocate, and no sin—no matter
how big or how frequent—is worth more than the
lifeblood of the spotless Lamb of God who poured
Himself out on the cross. He is the propitiation for our
sins. The Spirit speaks today of His sacrifice and the
cleansing power of His blood. It's not about how much
sorrow you feel, how much you weep, or how hard you
grit your teeth.

You cannot weep enough for your sin. Your sin is worth more tears than you could ever shed, and there's no way that you can repent "enough." You can't earn forgiveness or real repentance by tears or by hours of prayer. Your forgiveness and freedom from the grief and shame of your sin was purchased in full on Calvary's cross.

Today you are given repentance by grace and by the work of the Holy Spirit, not by your work. You just have to be sincere, believe, and receive His work and His surgery on your heart. You may have a deep, powerful, and agonizing repentance experience, or you may not. You may have a simple joy and knowledge that you are free. Let the Holy Spirit do His work. Listen to His voice and respond in love and faith.

> **Hebrews 4:6-7** – Since therefore it remains that some must enter it, and those to whom it was first preached did not enter because of disobedience, again He designates a certain day, saying in David, "Today," after such a long time, as it has been said: "Today, if you will hear His voice do not harden your hearts."

If the Spirit of God is speaking to you, convicting you of sin, do not harden your heart. Hear His voice. Don't run from the Father. He loves you. Crawl into His lap and ask Him to father you. Ask Him to restore you. Ask Him to wash you clean, to make you new, and to restore you in the truth of who you are.

ACTION STEP

Ask God:

Am I bearing the fruit of repentance that You desire in my life? What specific fruit is Your life producing in me as Your branch?

What are You saying to my heart about repentance? Is there something You have been trying to tell me, but my heart has been hard?

Pray through the fruit of godly sorrow:

1. "Diligence"
Lord, what does this look like in my life? What do You desire me to be diligent in?

2. "Clearing of yourselves" (of guilt, sin, and accusation)
Father, what should this look like in my life? Is there any action that I need to take to remove any tolerance of sin or accusation in my life?

3. "Indignation"
Father, what should this look like? Help me to be indignant toward even the suggestion that I should sin.

4. "Fear"
Lord, what should this look like in my life? Help me to hate sin and understand the seriousness of sin.

5. "Vehement desire"
Father give me this vehement desire for practical righteousness and holy living.

6. "Zeal"

Father, I want to have a passion for You. Is there passion lacking in my life? What would daily life look like if I had all the zeal You want for me?

7. "Vindication"

Father, thank you for your vindication. Help me trust your saving and keeping grace. I trust You, to help me walk forward in a way that vindicates and demonstrates who I am in You.

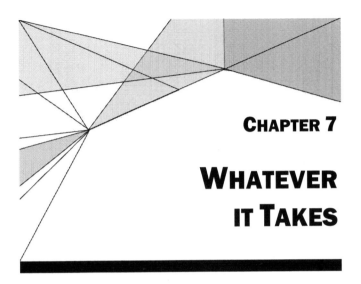

CHAPTER 7

WHATEVER
IT TAKES

My brother, a man whose generosity blesses many people, gave me a brand new laptop for my birthday. This gift was exactly what I needed, but it was also a danger to me.

I called my friend Neil and asked him, "Do you need a laptop?"

"Actually we do," he said. He was amazed at the timing and the magnitude of the gift. He asked me, "How did God tell you to give this to me?"

"A sudden conviction," I said.

I had just been set free from pornography and did not want to go back. I did not want the opportunity to go back. I did not want the possibility of going back. I didn't have Internet at my house, but my laptop picked up Internet from the neighbors. I wanted to be done. I would be fine without Internet at home for a while. I gave the laptop away.

> **Matthew 5:27-30** – "You have heard that it was said to those of old, 'You shall not commit adultery.' But I say to you that whoever looks at a woman to lust for her has already committed adultery with her in his heart. If your right eye causes you to sin, pluck it out and cast it from you; for it is more profitable for you that one of your members perish, than for your whole body to be cast into hell. And if your right hand causes you to sin, cut it off and cast it from you; for it is more profitable for you that one of your members perish, than for your whole body to be cast into hell."

I have heard Jesus's teaching in the Sermon on the Mount, and this passage in particular, maligned as having no application for believers today. This teaching appears multiple times in the Gospels, and we must acknowledge it on a very basic level.

It is true. It is true that it is better to lose an arm than to lose heaven. It is better to lose an eyeball than to go to hell. It is better to cut off any cause of sin than to lose eternity with Jesus.

This teaching starts off in the context of lust and adultery and then moves to an intense and difficult point. Do our hands cause us to sin? Do our eyes cause us to sin? No. Jesus clearly taught that sin comes from the heart (Matthew 15:19). From the heart we use our eyes and hands to sin. The heart is the root cause, but Jesus teaches us to cut off any opportunity for sin in our lives. His voice and word teach us to do whatever it takes to be free from sin.

We struggle with this teaching because, to many of

us, it doesn't sound like Jesus. He's talking about hell to people who intend to follow Him (study shows that this is often the audience for Jesus's many teachings on hell). He's connecting sinful behavior to hell; and rather than teaching about faith and the Holy Spirit, He teaches an extreme practical application.

We want to filter this out as something that Jesus wouldn't say to us. This is part of the prophetic—hearing things from Jesus we don't want to hear, listening to Jesus as He really is rather than as we want Him to be. If we are going to follow Jesus, we have to hear the rebuke and the hard saying.

Jesus still warns of hell, and Jesus still tells us to abstain from opportunities to sin. Jesus used extreme examples here to illustrate what is at stake. Holiness is who we are. Holy living is where we are and where we are going. If we reject holiness, we reject Jesus. Many live in brokenness and find themselves unable to find freedom. None of us have attained perfection, and we all lean on the grace and mercy of God. But Jesus commands us to do whatever it takes to find practical freedom and wholeness.

We have to apply this with the help of the Holy Spirit. I believe that giving away my new laptop was an act of faith and obedience. Maiming myself would not be. Maiming myself would say that I do not believe holiness is available or attainable as God created me. Giving away my laptop, however, says that I am willing to do whatever it takes to be free and that I am taking steps to spend time away from temptation. I have Internet at my house now, and if someone gave me another laptop, I would keep it. For that season, giving away the laptop was the right thing to do.

Paul wrote, "But put on the Lord Jesus Christ, and make no provision for the flesh, to fulfill its lusts" (Romans 13:14). Paul's teaching parallels Christ's. We are commanded to cut off opportunities to sin and to fulfill lusts. We must avoid those areas. We must not "make provision" for the flesh. This means we should not provide ourselves with an opportunity, with the tools, with the situation, with the scenario to fulfill our lusts. We are to ask God to "lead us not into temptation," and we are to live consistent with that by avoiding temptation ourselves.

In 2 Timothy 2:22, Paul ordered Timothy to "flee from youthful lusts," not to fight them. When it comes to temptation and sinful desire, we should run like Joseph ran from Potiphar's wife (Genesis 39:12). We must flee from the situation and avoid it rather than trusting in our own strength or entering a long battle of will with temptation. We will have opportunities to resist the devil and temptation even if we live in perfect wisdom.

Parodies of this teaching exist everywhere from the Amish subculture to warnings of "don't drink, dance, or chew, and don't spend time with those who do." Holiness is being separated from this world's system and keeping ourselves unspotted from the world, but you must have contact with the world to be salt and light. This involves many decisions of individual conscience and the application of wisdom. We must let God speak to us in these areas. Without His voice sending us into the world, we can become irrelevant to our neighbors. Without His voice calling us away from temptation, we can be ensnared.

There are those who can do things that I cannot do because I am tempted in areas that they are not and vice versa. There are times when the Holy Spirit does lead us into temptation (Jesus in the wilderness), and in those times we must be obedient and trust the same Spirit to keep us. As far as it is up to us, we are meant to avoid temptation and do whatever it takes to live in freedom.

Later in Matthew Jesus repeated the same teaching from the Sermon on the Mount:

> **Matthew 18:8-9** – "If your hand or foot causes you to sin, cut it off and cast it from you. It is better for you to enter into life lame or maimed, rather than having two hands or two feet, to be cast into the everlasting fire. And if your eye causes you to sin, pluck it out and cast it from you. It is better for you to enter into life with one eye, rather than having two eyes, to be cast into hell fire.

This was something that Jesus taught multiple times to multiple crowds. Those who are weak, those who are struggling, those who are caught in the same bondage again and again, should listen carefully. It is time to take whatever practical steps are necessary to find freedom from the cycle of sin and shame that destroys faith.

It is better to be without Internet than to be addicted to pornography. It is better to quit your job than to have an affair with a co-worker. It is better to find accountability and counseling than to continue in an eating disorder. It is better to go to detox than continue doing drugs.

God has an instantaneous miracle for each of us. He has finished the work on the cross. It is our responsibility to walk according to our faith and steward what he has given us. Physical boundaries and cutting off the opportunity to sin provides a break from addiction cycles and time for our brains, bodies, and souls to reset from the damaging patterns we have created.

The practical cutting off of opportunity to sin also demonstrates genuine repentance. We aren't fooling ourselves or making subconscious plans to go back to our sin. We are physically and practically demonstrating our repentance by making a decision outside of temptation that will minimize temptation in our lives. This can be an act of faith.

> **Mark 9:42-50** – "But whoever causes one of these little ones who believe in Me to stumble, it would be better for him if a millstone were hung around his neck, and he were thrown into the sea.
>
> "If your hand causes you to sin, cut it off. It is better for you to enter into life maimed, rather than having two hands, to go to hell, into the fire that shall never be quenched—where 'Their worm does not die, and the fire is not quenched.'
>
> "And if your foot causes you to sin, cut it off. It is better for you to enter life lame, rather than having two feet, to be cast into hell, into the fire that shall never be quenched—where 'Their worm does not die, and the fire is not quenched.' And if your eye causes you to sin, pluck it out. It is better for you to enter the kingdom of God with one eye, rather than having two eyes, to be cast into hell fire—where 'Their worm does not die, and the fire is not

quenched.'

"For everyone will be seasoned with fire,
and every sacrifice will be seasoned with salt.
Salt is good, but if the salt loses its flavor, how
will you season it? Have salt in yourselves, and
have peace with one another."

Mark Chapter Nine features some of Jesus's harshest teaching regarding hell. I have no doubt that if Jesus was walking the earth and taught this today, He would come under severe criticism. Just reading this Scripture draws criticism these days. It seems we do not want the fear or wrath of God mentioned.

Jesus must bring up hell and fear as motivations because we are often so immature in love that righteousness and repentance must be motivated by our own self-interest and fear.

All parents want their children to obey them out of love, but every parent knows that, in their children's immaturity, fear of punishment and consequences is often a more effective motivation for obedience. Parents will use punishment to motivate their children to stay away from harm and keep them safe. So will God.

1 John 4:18 – There is no fear in love. But
perfect love drives out fear, because fear has to
do with punishment. The one who fears is not
made perfect in love. (NIV)

When we are made perfect in love, when love is our true and overwhelming motivation, and when we love perfectly and receive perfect love from the Father—there will be no need for fear. Until that day, the fear of the

113

Lord will be present in our lives, and it should be strongest in the immature and disobedient.

Until we recognize God's discipline as love and obey from the love that's in our hearts, fear of eternal consequences will and should be present in our lives. Destruction and death are the consequences of sin. Sin cannot be taken lightly. Jesus died for our freedom from sin. God paid the highest price to destroy sin in our lives and save us from the world, the flesh, and the devil.

It may seem like I have an axe to grind with these verses, and I do. I have experienced addiction, and I have worked with many others who have been bound by addiction as well. I have worked with those addicted to pornography, drugs, and sex with strangers. Some of them would be alive today if they had done whatever it took to be free. If they would have taken desperate measures to cut themselves off from heroin, they would be alive. They didn't, and they're gone.

Addiction and sin have a way of warping our minds. I'm always amazed at the pride I could walk in while being addicted to pornography. I had lost the ability to be truly honest with myself. God's voice had to cut through the haze of rationalization and lies to set me free.

Deception and self-deception are always components of addiction. Whether it's drugs, pornography, or losing your temper, cycles of sin blind us. It becomes painful to admit the truth about ourselves and our behavior, and rather than face that pain with honesty, we manage to push the truth away and find ways to justify and rationalize our behavior. This prevents us from taking the necessary steps to be free.

True repentance and cutting ourselves off from the

opportunities to fulfill lusts and addictive behaviors requires honesty about our past and present. It is surprising to look back at all the tears I shed and all the agony I went through trying to find repentance from pornography—yet how few practical steps I attempted.

We subconsciously have ways to rationalize staying in situations that allow us to fulfill our lusts and sinful desires. Deep in our hearts we know that if we really wanted to be free we would cut off access to the fulfillment of our sinful desires. If we really wanted to be free we would cut off the Internet, install a filter, cut off a relationship, tell a friend, ask for help, or do any number of other things to "make no provision for the flesh."

Faith cannot be separated from obedient action. Faith that we can and will be free cannot be separated from practical, obedient action to be free. This obedient action also demonstrates the desire of one's heart. It expresses that beyond comfort, beyond pain, beyond looking good, we desire repentance and freedom.

> **Galatians 3:1-7 –** O foolish Galatians! Who has bewitched you that you should not obey the truth, before whose eyes Jesus Christ was clearly portrayed among you as crucified? This only I want to learn from you: Did you receive the Spirit by the works of the law, or by the hearing of faith? Are you so foolish? Having begun in the Spirit, are you now being made perfect by the flesh? Have you suffered so many things in vain—if indeed it was in vain?
>
> Therefore He who supplies the Spirit to you and works miracles among you, does He do it by the works of the law, or by the hearing of

faith?—just as Abraham "believed God, and it was accounted to him for righteousness." Therefore know that only those who are of faith are sons of Abraham.

There remains an ongoing tension between works and faith. This tension exists in our justification and in our sanctification and transformation. While we are commanded to do whatever it takes to be free, we know that whatever is not of faith is sin (Romans 14:23).

Making no provision for the flesh, cutting off opportunities to sin, and staying away from temptation in itself will not make you holy. It is not the answer. It is not what will complete you in Christ. It is not freedom. Christ's finished work is freedom. Christ's transformation of the heart is freedom. The blood of Jesus and the Spirit of God are what perfect and complete us. We are transformed by the Spirit, not by our works. It is foolishness and false teaching to believe that we can be made righteous or holy by what we do. This even applies to Christ's commands.

Cutting off access to the Internet for the rest of your life does not necessarily mean that you are holy. We do whatever it takes because of and as part of the Spirit's work in our lives. We do it because we have been made free to make this choice. We do it because God touched our hearts. We do it as part of obedience to the Spirit's work. These practical applications are not *the* answer, and Jesus did not say that they were. We are to do them as a part of experiencing that transformation.

The Red Sea didn't part until Moses stretched his staff over it. The walls of Jericho didn't fall without a lot of disciplined, silent marching followed by a shout. God gave Joshua victory over the Amalekites, but only when Moses's arms were raised. His shoulders became tired and Aaron and Hur had to hold his hands up. We have our part to play in the working of a miracle. Practical effort partners with the miraculous power of God to provide supernatural paths of deliverance, to tear down walls, and to provide the victory. God rarely does the miracle without you.

"I say then: Walk in the Spirit, and you shall not fulfill the lust of the flesh" (Galatians 5:16). The way to freedom and a holy life is to walk and live in the Spirit and His desires. The Holy Spirit and His direction, leading, and desire within us conform us to the life and character of Christ. This is the goal. This is the end-state—to look like Jesus.

We have to acknowledge that in our daily life on earth, we don't always look like Jesus. We fail. We experience brokenness. Because of this, we must go through the experience of confession, cleansing, and repentance—a process Jesus did not have to go through in the same way. We must allow the Holy Spirit to deal with us in this process and allow the perfection of faith to have its way. There are different measures of faith and different applications as well. Some people are instantly and miraculously delivered from addiction. Many more find grace and faith in the process of walking out repentance, rejecting lies, and experiencing truth in the Holy Spirit. This process often includes cutting off opportunities for the weakness of our flesh and avoiding sin and temptation.

Our pride often says that we don't have to do that— that we have great faith–that we can believe for a miracle—that we are not really doing that badly anyway.

And so we dodge the work the Spirit wants to do in our lives.

Often we are so bound by self-deception and imprisoned to our own lusts and desires that we struggle to hear and experience the Holy Spirit and the path to freedom. Cutting ourselves off from the opportunity to fulfill the desires of the flesh gives us time to rise above the cloud of deception and see clearly. Such practical restraints grant us a moment of clarity. We find faith as we practically obey Jesus. We find freedom because we actually do something that demonstrates the fruit of repentance. We find the truth because we are honest about our weakness.

If you are in bondage today, ask the Holy Spirit what provisions you have made for your flesh; and by His leading, cut those things off. Do it by faith in His work, and trust that it will lead you to greater freedom.

ACTION STEP

Ask God:

Have I made any provision for the flesh in my life?

Is there anything I need to do to cut off the opportunity to sin?

Have I intentionally walked into or lived in temptation?

Is there anything that I haven't done that deep down I know I would do if I really wanted to be free?

What is Your way of escape for me?

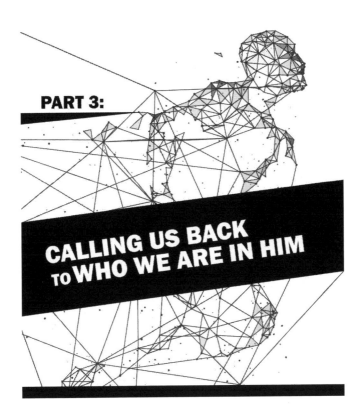

PART 3:

CALLING US BACK TO WHO WE ARE IN HIM

God reveals our identity in Christ through relationship with Him. As we grow in Him and in His family, He establishes and reminds us of who we are. He tells us that we are His sons, that we are holy, and that we are accepted.

Knowing our identity in Christ empowers us to live holy lives. God's voice reveals who we are in Christ in a way that goes beyond words on a page or simple knowledge. He makes it real to us in relationship with Him.

God still reminds me of who I am in Him. I am still learning and growing up into all that God has done. The following explains who we are in Christ and how God reveals that to us. How God reveals who we are in Him is different for each person. The revelation of His completed work is just as powerful whether received in a quiet moment with the Bible or a powerful vision from above. I hope the following reminds you of what God has already been speaking to your heart.

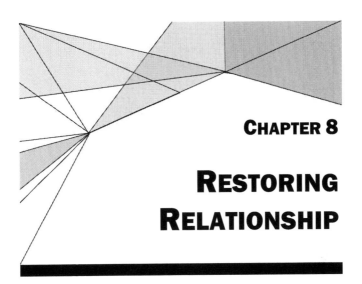

CHAPTER 8

RESTORING
RELATIONSHIP

Shortly after I was born again, I became involved in the campus ministry at my university. I was young, immature, full of pride, and legalistic; but I had zeal and a passionate love for God. My pride and legalism caused me to clash often with other members of the campus ministry and the leaders.

After a year or so, I became part of the leadership team, but I struggled immensely with a sister in the Lord who was one of the leaders. In my arrogance I labeled her as the root of all the problems in the ministry. God would not allow me to stay in my pride and ignorance.

I used to walk laps around the campus while I was praying. In many ways I didn't know how to pray, but I was spending time with the Lord, learning to be intimate with Him, and learning to intercede. Each lap would take 45 minutes to an hour depending on which route I took and how fast I walked. At one point as I went out to walk, I heard God tell me to pray for this sister. I did not want to pray for her. I did not like her. But I was obedient to the Lord. Somehow I figured out how to pray for her for the whole lap. I was probably very pharisaical and sanctimonious in my prayers, but I managed to string enough together to make it through. After I finished the lap I thought, "Now I can really pray."

But God said, "Pray for her again." So I took another lap, running out of words this time and mostly just praying in the Spirit with this sister on my mind. I finished worn out and ready to stop, but God said, "Pray for her again."

I began to cry. I walked a third lap praying through a lump in my throat. Suddenly she really had become my sister. For months I would start out my prayer times by taking time to specifically pray for this sister, and throughout my time in college she was one of the people I carried to the throne of grace on a regular basis—not because I loved her but because Jesus did, and somehow in that time of prayer He gave me His heart for her.

A few years later, this sister made a major mistake. Her mistake happened publically and created a huge interpersonal problem that included many people in the campus ministry.

The night it happened I stayed up praying and crying. I still don't know if I've ever felt the burden of the Lord so strongly for an individual. Somehow, I knew that this sister was considering walking away from the campus ministry and the church. I was completely at a loss. I cried and prayed in tongues for hours.

What hurt even more was that I was to be blamed in part for the incident. Others claimed that the incident escalated and occurred because of my sinful judgment and legalism. And perhaps it did. I had been struggling on and off with pornography addiction at that point and certainly was not in any place to judge. In the severe grief of it all, I wrote a letter to this sister, and in it I discovered and spoke from the heart of God in a way I never had before.

Many may look at the words and wonder where the great revelation was. This would be a prophetic baby step for many, and it was for me as well, but I still look back at it as one of the most important personal prophecies I've ever given.

Dear [Sister],

Beyond all the pressures and struggles of this world, God's love remains unfailing and unchanging. In His eyes you are the beautiful woman He knew when He formed you. His grace and favor do not waver or change. It is not up or down, or in and out. It is a constant love for His daughter.

He knows where you've been, and He knows what you've done. He knows all the things that have made you who you are. He sees all the failures and all the successes. He sees all the weaknesses and all the strengths. And in the midst of it all, He wants you to know that you are beautiful to Him and that He's working in you to change the failures to blessings, the weaknesses to strengths, and the loneliness to unfailing love.

This college world is filled with cunningly devised fables, lies, and confusing schemes; but in the midst of it all God is working to meet you where you are, touch your heart, and give you an unshakeable experience with the truth of His love—not because of what you've done or not done, but because of who you are: His beautiful child.

Through tough times and heartache, He is there, experiencing the burden for the child He loves. Though He may seem far away,

He is speaking to let you know that He'll always love you, and nothing you could ever do could make Him love you less. It's this love that works in your brothers and sisters. He has placed people around you, not for judgment or correction but because He is working in their hearts to bind them close to you and provide support.

In that we fail—in our flesh and weakness—but even in our failures, we have you in our hearts. Because you are beautiful to us. You are a sister who cannot be replaced, someone we love dearly. At times we may seem prickly or uncaring, but we really just want to express the unconditional love that God has placed in our hearts. And it is unconditional. In the same way that God could never love you less, so, too, are we unable to ever love you less. If you were to leave us all and choose never to speak to us again, we would still cherish you in our hearts because you are our sister, and we know the beauty of your heart.

We know it because we have been with you through thick and thin, and you have been with us. It is this love that perseveres, and I know that this love will persevere in you. I can see beyond anything that happens that God is making you the woman that He wants you to be, and I cannot ignore the love that he has placed in my heart for you, my sister.

-Jonathan

She said she had been planning to leave the campus ministry, and that the letter shook her and brought her back. It was not because I called out her sin, called her to greater holiness, or revealed intimate knowledge of her life or impressive revelation that only God could know but because I revealed the heart of God that restores us all as His children.

During times of brokenness, shame, and despair God speaks into our lives with incredible power, restoring us back to relationship with Him and empowering us to walk in His love. When we're sick from the poison of lies, He speaks the truth of His unconditional love and His transforming grace. When we hear Him speak, our lives conform to the power of His Word.

When God thinks of you, He thinks in mercy. He doesn't remember you according to your sins (Psalm 25:7; Hebrews 8:12). He thinks of you with compassion and grace. He sympathizes with your weakness and your pain. He has valued you at the price of His own Son's life. The precious blood of Jesus is more valuable and speaks clearer and louder than any sin you could ever commit (Hebrews 12:24).

God's desire for relationship with you goes to the point of shedding perfect blood. He humbled Himself, entered the body of an infant, lived out all the experience of human weakness and pain, gave His life in service, and then died a criminal's death so that He could have an unbroken relationship with you. When sin and fear break that relationship, He still pursues you as a Father, desperate to bring you back into His arms and restore you in His love. Like the father of the prodigal son, He runs to you (Luke 15).

Even the lukewarm Church of Laodicea received an invitation to intimacy and fellowship with Jesus. Though they were stagnant and lost in failure and sin, Jesus said, "Here I am! I stand at the door and knock. If anyone hears my voice and opens the door, I will come in and eat with that person, and they with me" (Revelation 3:20 NIV). Even when we are in sin, Jesus desires us. He calls to us and knocks on the door of our heart, willing and ready to enter our lives and fellowship with us in intimacy and love.

About a year after the love and fear of the Lord set me free from pornography, I went to see another itinerant minister with some friends. He preached a powerful message on redemption. Since my experience with God's deep conviction that set me free from pornography, I often felt fear when I sensed the intense and powerful presence of the Holy Spirit upon a speaker. It reminded me of the paralyzing conviction that I went through the previous year. In many ways I have never gotten over that experience with the fear of the Lord, and in some ways I hope I never do. The minister gave a powerful altar call for those who were suffering in their bodies because of past sins. He passionately explained the injustice of carrying any disease or penalty for sin in your body when Jesus carried the penalty for sin in His, and he added,

> You got marks on your body from misconduct; there was a time when you didn't see your value, and you cut yourself. Why don't we just pray that Jesus takes that away and puts a brand new skin graft over it? If you hurt yourself, I want you to come up here, and I want to lay hands on you and command that thing to go.

I still had scars on my body from putting matches out on myself and cutting myself before I knew the Lord, so I responded and went to the altar hoping that my scars would be washed away by the hand of Christ, but secretly I was trembling inside. Would my sin be called out again? I was trying to remember the last time I had fallen into lust. The minister was prophesying over people as he prayed for the healing. When he came to me, he put his hand on my head and immediately said,

> Son. You are forgiven. I heard that as soon as I
> touched you. Now be whole in your body.

My scars didn't disappear, but my soul was healed. I was forgiven. I came to the altar struggling with condemnation, crying out to God on the inside, God have mercy, and I walked away knowing that I was justified in God's eyes.

Never underestimate forgiveness, and never underestimate the power of prophesying forgiveness and love to others. It may be general. It may not impress anyone. But it heals the heart, and it has the ability to transform lives.

Peter stated that one of the reasons people continue in sin is because they forget that they've been cleansed from their former sins (2 Peter 1:9). They forget. They don't hold onto the knowledge and truth of forgiveness and cleansing. That certainty and faith in the blood of Jesus and the power of His forgiveness keeps us holy and reveals the love of Jesus.

When the sinful woman came to anoint Jesus's feet in Luke Chapter Seven, the Pharisees struggled to believe in Christ's prophetic call and abilities. Surely this woman was worthy of shunning, of casting out, of rebuking, and condemning. Jesus challenged their concept of love and forgiveness, forever revealing the heart of the Father.

We don't know how the woman came to find out about Jesus. Perhaps she was the woman caught in adultery in John 8. Perhaps she was simply walking by and heard Jesus teaching about forgiveness and grace. Perhaps He had treated her with love and respect.

We don't have that part of the story, but we do know that she saw something in Jesus. She saw love and grace. Here was this eminent teacher, prophet, and Messiah, and she saw Him stoop down for the outcast. She saw Him love the oppressed, heal the leper, and have compassion on the sinner and the failure. He called the castaways of society and lifted them into disciples of the Son of God. She saw Him as worthy of worship. She loved Him.

We don't know how she found out where Jesus was staying, but we know that she barged into a Pharisee's home. She entered the place where she was despised and where she found reproach. She risked humiliation, exposure, and rejection to get to Jesus. When she got to the Master, she fell at His feet and began to worship Him with tears. She washed His feet with her tears and her hair. She took the lowest part of Jesus and made it an altar. She went into the dust to lift Jesus in the sight of all.

Simon the Pharisee wondered why Jesus allowed her to touch Him, and Jesus, knowing Simon's thoughts, answered by explaining why this woman worshipped Him so:

> **Luke 7:41-48 –** There was a certain creditor who had two debtors. One owed five hundred denarii, and the other fifty. And when they had nothing with which to repay, he freely forgave them both. Tell Me, therefore, which of them will love him more?
>
> Simon answered and said, "I suppose the one whom he forgave more."
>
> And He said to him, "You have rightly judged." Then He turned to the woman and said to Simon, "Do you see this woman? I entered your house; you gave Me no water for My feet, but she has washed My feet with her tears and

wiped them with the hair of her head. You gave
Me no kiss, but this woman has not ceased to
kiss My feet since the time I came in. You did
not anoint My head with oil, but this woman has
anointed My feet with fragrant oil. Therefore I
say to you, her sins, which are many, are
forgiven, for she loved much. But to whom little
is forgiven, the same loves little."

Then He said to her, "Your sins are
forgiven."

This woman was motivated by love. She loved Jesus
because she had grasped the forgiveness He offered. She
understood the vast debt that He had erased. She had seen
her filth and sin. She had experienced the rejection and
pain of her sin. She was vile in the eyes of society, in the
eyes of the law, in the eyes of the religious, and she
thought she was vile in the eyes of God.

But here was the voice of God, telling her that she
was valuable, that she was forgiven, that she was not
condemned. It turned her life upside-down, and she burst
through boundaries, taboos, and social structures, risking
herself in order to get to Jesus and worship Him. She who
is forgiven much loves much.

I once asked God about this verse. It didn't seem
fair to me. The worst sinners become the greatest lovers?
How was that fair? Didn't God value righteousness and
holiness? I had no argument with God. I knew I had been
a filthy sinner. I had defiled God in my mind and heart in
every way that I knew how when I was running from God.
But it seemed so unjust that those who lived righteous
lives would lack the love that great forgiveness gave.

God reminded me, "There is not one who is

righteous, no not one" (Romans 3:10). "For whoever keeps the whole law and yet stumbles at just one point is guilty of breaking all of it" (James 2:10). Suddenly I realized we have all been forgiven the same amount. We are all guilty of the life and blood of Jesus Christ. We all put Him on the cross. Those of us who experienced the deep sin may understand that better and may have an easier time realizing the vastness of how much we've been forgiven, but the revelation of incredible, life-changing forgiveness is available to all.

The revelation of forgiveness changes our lives and produces love. Take some time to remember how much you have been forgiven and worship Him there. He loved you. He forgave you. Before we believed it, before we knew Him, God demonstrated His great love for us by sending His Son to die for us (Romans 5:8). We love Him because He loved us first (1 John 4:19). Your forgiveness was purchased. Your redemption was paid for. He loves you. You are forgiven. His voice is speaking, applying His forgiveness to your failure and sowing love into your heart.

God's voice calls us to run to Him—not run from Him. If we were to see in the Spirit, we would see Him running to us. God paid the highest price for a relationship with you. No sin is worth more than that. If you desire a relationship with Him, He desires it more: and He runs to you with love, ready to restore all that you had before. He's ready to apply His redemptive plan, which, beyond comprehension, is never second best.

ACTION STEP

In this action step, you are going to ask God questions to which you almost certainly already know the answer. The questions are there so that you can hear God say them and listen to how and what He says about them. Let God speak to you.

Ask God:

God, do You love me?

How much?

Do You forgive me?

How much?

Will You always be with me?

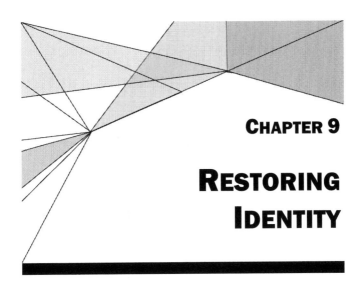

CHAPTER 9

RESTORING IDENTITY

The summer after I was born again, I spent a lot of time walking up and down the private road where my parents' house is. I remember one evening walking through the rows of trees with a cold pit of hopelessness in my stomach. I had just fallen into pornography, and as a young believer my faith was weak.

I was praying frantically, wondering if God would forgive me, when a sharp voice said, "I'm going to make you an intercessor."

I spun around to see who had spoken, but no one was there. It was one of the few times in my life that I've heard the audible voice of God. It wasn't during a time of intense worship in the presence of God. It wasn't because I had climbed Mount Sinai or ascended to the third heaven to hear unspeakable things. I had just watched pornography.

God's forgiveness and restoration are far beyond what we expect. He loves to restore. He loves to make us new. He loves to remind us of our future. He speaks to us of His eternal love and our eternal value. He loves to remind us of our hope.

Where there is no prophetic vision the people cast off restraint (Proverbs 29:18). One of the purposes of God's voice and the prophetic is to show us a vision and a hope that restrains us from sin in the present and moves us into the future.

We know that sin can wreak havoc with the plan God has for us. Keeping a prophetic vision in sight enables us to walk in the strength of that vision. By showing me a picture of my calling and future, the Father gave me a powerful restraint against sin and a powerful motivation for holiness.

For the next four years I learned how to intercede, and I functioned as an intercessor in the ministry. I spent hours everyday praying for others. I continued in this practice until entering full-time ministry when God began to put the work of an evangelist on my heart.

God has spoken this kind of restoration to me many times. I often spent many hours in prayer after falling into sin, seeking repentance and restoration. I remember a very specific moment lying on the carpet for hours, shattered by my sin and my double mindedness and trying to find a shred of hope that I could change.

As I lay there, my body became paralyzed, and I went into a vision. I was looking out into a vast, sandy desert. In the center of the wasteland was a burning bush. It was a steady, burning flame filled with the subtle glow of God. The bush was not consumed.

Moses then stood before the bush, sandals discarded in the presence of the voice of the Lord and in the knowledge that he stood on holy ground. I appeared in the scene. I watched myself walk slowly past Moses as if I were invisible, step into the center of the burning bush, and disappear into the glow and flame of God. The bush began to vibrate with God's voice, and the vision faded.

Moses was called to approach God and stand on holy ground. By the blood of Jesus we stand there, too. But unlike Moses, we can freely and boldly approach the throne of grace. We are hidden in Christ. Moses stood before the burning bush. We stand in Christ—hidden in His holiness and love, protected by His blood and His mercy. We have been accepted in the beloved (Ephesians 1:6).

I wish I could say that these experiences ended my pornography addiction as God intended or that they cut off my struggles with lust. They didn't. I fell again.

The voice of God invites us to holiness, but it doesn't force it on us. God offered me freedom again and again, but because of my own double-mindedness and hardness of heart, I turned away from freedom. I believe that it was likely because I had been given such grace and truth that God finally dealt so harshly with me when I was set free. But I'll never forget the powerful restoration and hope that those experiences with the voice of God sowed into my heart. God does not shun darkness or failure. He speaks into it.

WHAT DO WE DO NOW?

As I was preparing to preach about obedience at a Sunday-morning service at my home church, God kept speaking to me about John 21 instead. I felt that I had the right message for that morning, but I also knew that God wanted to add something. I put John 21 as the first thing to speak about and decided to allow the Holy Spirit the opportunity to speak prophetically.

That Saturday night the Holy Spirit got me out of bed at midnight to study John 21. I jotted down some notes and arrived that morning with a strong anticipation. After preaching on the passage for a few minutes the Holy Spirit moved me into prophecy. The leaders of the church were moved to tears, and the whole church went into a time of spontaneous worship before I was able to preach the message on obedience and see two people make Jesus their Lord for the first time. God's voice works wonders.

John 21 is a story of failure, disappointment, redemption, and restoration. Jesus had gone to the cross and died for you and me. He had risen from the dead, and He had shown Himself to His disciples. They knew that He was alive, but they'd not yet experienced Pentecost.

It was a time of great transition and testing for the disciples. They were bewildered and confused. They were struggling with personal guilt. They had abandoned Jesus. They had scattered and run like cowards. Their faith had been demolished by fear. They had all denied Jesus in their actions, and Peter had denied Jesus with His mouth. They were no longer physically present with Jesus day by day. Now Jesus was alive, but how were they to recover? How could they come back to a healthy relationship with Him and look Him in the eye when they still felt the shame of their sin?

Times of transition and testing can be tough on our faith. But there is a word of wisdom: Though a righteous man falls seven times, he gets back up (Proverbs 24:16). When we're waiting for God to restore us, it may be hard to rise and believe in God's great mercy.

Times of failure reveal where our heart and faith are. Do we believe that God is going to be faithful? Do we believe that God is going to be true? Do we have our eyes fixed on Jesus? Or do we feel like God has abandoned us?

The disciples struggled with feeling abandoned. They felt like Jesus had left them; He was alive, but He was no longer walking with them as He had before. They may have wondered if they were being rejected because of their sin. They were dealing with confusion. They had still hoped that Jesus was going to win an earthly kingdom, but now they weren't sure what to think. They didn't know if the plan Jesus had promised was still intact or if it had been irreparably damaged by their cowardice.

They didn't know what to do. So they decided to go back to what they knew. They decided to return to what they were doing before they met Jesus. They decided to go fishing.

Perhaps they even decided to go back to their old identities and become fishermen, rather than fishers of men.

This happens to us, too. After a failure, the enemy comes to tempt us to own our actions as our identities and to fall back and embrace who we were before we met Jesus. We struggle and identify ourselves with our past. We try to hold onto what Christ has made us. We have to fight to see our identities in Christ because the enemy is attempting to use sin to cloud our eyes.

John 21:1-4 – ...after these things Jesus showed Himself again to the disciples at the Sea of Tiberias, and in this way He showed Himself:

139

> Simon Peter, Thomas called the Twin, Nathanael
> of Cana in Galilee, the sons of Zebedee, and two
> others of His disciples were together. Simon
> Peter said to them, "I am going fishing."
>
> They said to him, "We are going with you
> also." They went out and immediately got into
> the boat, and that night they caught nothing.
>
> But when the morning had now come, Jesus
> stood on the shore; yet the disciples did not
> know that it was Jesus.

Times of failure, transition, and restoration are times of encounter with Jesus. He might seem far away, and you might not see Him or know that He's there. You might not recognize Him, but He is standing on the shore calling to you.

> **John 21:5-6 –** Then Jesus said to them,
> "Children, have you any food?"
>
> They answered Him, "No."
>
> And He said to them, "Cast the net on the
> right side of the boat, and you will find some."
> So they cast, and now they were not able to
> draw it in because of the multitude of fish.

Times of failure, transition, and restoration are times of provision. They are times when God desires to give you the strength and the resources to succeed where you once failed. God wants to restore your abilities in Him. He wants to feed you and sustain you with His Word and His voice. He desires to bring you from a place where you do not have enough to a place where there is more than enough. He wants to move you from a place where you cannot provide for yourself to a place where He provides for you. He desires to move us from working in our own strength and weakness to working in His infinite strength and power. Feel free to stop reading and ask the Lord to take you through this change-process. Right now.

When Jesus walks with us, He is always taking us to a better place. He gives us something to do, and He instructs us in the supernatural. When we obey we find all that we need. He told the disciples, "Cast the net on the right side of the boat, and you will find some [fish]." He gave them a prophetic word that redirected their human effort into a supernatural effort. Times of restoration are times to listen and obey as Jesus gives us directions for success and victory.

> **John 21:7 –** Therefore that disciple whom Jesus loved said to Peter, "It is the Lord!" Now when Simon Peter heard that it was the Lord, he put on his outer garment (for he had removed it), and plunged into the sea.

Times of transition and restoration are times of revelation. You will see Jesus in a way that you have never seen Him before. You are given a revelation of who and where Jesus is. The disciples were going through a time where they couldn't understand or see what Jesus was doing, but here He appeared on the shore, still providing the miraculous.

Peter plunged into the sea to meet Him. During times of failure and transition we should aggressively cast everything aside and go to Jesus.

> **John 21:8-13 –** But the other disciples came in
> the little boat (for they were not far from land,
> but about two hundred cubits), dragging the net
> with fish. Then, as soon as they had come to
> land, they saw a fire of coals there, and fish laid
> on it, and bread. Jesus said to them, "Bring
> some of the fish which you have just caught."
> Simon Peter went up and dragged the net to
> land, full of large fish, one hundred and fifty-
> three; and although there were so many, the
> net was not broken. Jesus said to them, "Come
> and eat breakfast." Yet none of the disciples
> dared ask Him, "Who are You?"—knowing that
> it was the Lord. Jesus then came and took the
> bread and gave it to them, and likewise the fish.

Times of restoration are times of intimacy—a time
to eat with Jesus. Jesus gave an invitation to His disciples
to eat with Him. They may have been afraid that He would
bring up their failures or rebuke them saying, "How could
you desert Me like that?" Instead He came to fellowship
and to break bread with them.

> **John 21:15 –** So when they had eaten breakfast,
> Jesus said to Simon Peter, "Simon, son of Jonah,
> do you love Me more than these?"
> He said to Him, "Yes, Lord; You know that I
> love You."
> He said to him, "Feed My lambs."

Peter had denied Jesus three times vocally and
publicly. It hung as a heavy burden around his heart. He
was suffocating in the guilt and shame of what he had

done. It was the greatest sin any of the disciples could have imagined themselves committing, yet here Peter had proved himself a coward and lost everything he had once stood for.

I can imagine Peter thinking, Lord, I messed it up. I denied You. I lost everything. I failed. But what can I say Jesus? You know that I love You. You know that I love You.

And Jesus responded, "Feed My lambs." This confrontation of failure became a place of calling. Jesus gave Peter a calling and a mission. He prophetically put something on Peter's heart. He declared Peter as useful.

> **John 21:16-17 –** He said to him again a second time, "Simon, son of Jonah, do you love Me?" He said to Him, "Yes, Lord; You know that I love You."
>
> He said to him, "Tend My sheep."
>
> He said to him the third time, "Simon, son of Jonah, do you love Me?" Peter was grieved because He said to him the third time, "Do you love Me?"
>
> And he said to Him, "Lord, You know all things; You know that I love You."
>
> Jesus said to him, "Feed My sheep."

Peter's three denials were replaced with three confessions of love. It was not only a prophetic Word, it was a prophetic interaction in which Peter was able to participate. He was given the opportunity to change his confession and change his response.

The same is true when Jesus restores us. He gives us the opportunity to rewrite our character and rewrite the actions and words of failure. He opens a door back into our identity in Him and speaks the truth to guide us through that door of revelation.

Jesus moved Peter from a low place to a place of calling and power. He took the disciple who denied Him and made him an apostle in the Church. He took the failure and made him part of the foundation of what He was building on the earth.

> **John 21:18-19 –** Most assuredly, I say to you, when you were younger, you girded yourself and walked where you wished; but when you are old, you will stretch out your hands, and another will gird you and carry you where you do not wish." This He spoke, signifying by what death he would glorify God. And when He had spoken this, He said to him, "Follow Me."

Peter's place of failure became a place of revelation and vision. Jesus took this time when Peter's heart was tender and spoke to him of the future. He turned Peter's gaze from past failures to future victory. He spoke to Peter of suffering, but He reminded him of His calling and His love, empowering him to walk into his destiny and the perfect redemptive plan of God.

Jesus spoke to Peter and the disciples before He ascended, when the memory of the cross and their denial and desertion of Him was still fresh, saying "All authority in heaven and on earth has been given to Me; therefore go and make disciples of all nations, baptizing them in the name of the Father and of the Son and of the Holy Spirit, teaching them to obey everything that I taught you; and behold I am with you always even to the end of the age"

(Matthew 28:18-20).

Jesus gave them a mission and trusted them to carry it out. He told them that He was no longer going to be with them in the flesh but that He was giving them a mission and a calling and a future. He set their hearts on something to do for Him. He prophesied that He would use them to pour out His love on the world and show the world who He was. These deserters—these failures—became an army.

He instructed them to wait in Jerusalem because the most precious gift He could give after His life was coming. He was sending the Holy Spirit. These failed cowards would be clothed with power from on high. He restored them with power for a task. He didn't throw the disciples away. He didn't reject them. He didn't forsake them. He didn't punish them. He essentially said, "I still have a hope for you. I still have a plan for you. I still have a purpose for you. I still love you. I'm still after you. I value you. You are more important to Me than anything you've done."

In the same way that God does not overlook sin, He does not overlook our purpose and calling. He believes in us.

He calls us to repentance, which is not only a turning away from sin but a turning toward Him and His plan for our lives. His plan includes the glory of serving Him in love and power.

God chooses the weak, the broken, and the humble for His service. He calls confused and failing disciples to change the world and lead a movement that will never stop until the end of time. God restores us in our identity in Him as members of His body, as new creations, and as supernatural servants.

ACTION STEP

Ask God:

How do You see me?

Who am I?

What's Your vision for my life?

If this is true, how should I live? How do I walk into that? Where should I start?

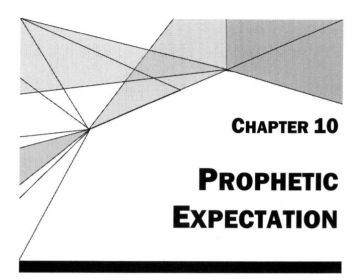

CHAPTER 10

PROPHETIC EXPECTATION

A s a child I once asked my father why I couldn't ask God to forgive me for all the sins I would ever commit. It seemed like it would save a lot of time and grief. After all, I already knew that God would forgive me later for sins I wanted to commit now. How was that different from knowing that I was already forgiven for all the future sins I would commit? I thought this preemptive forgiveness idea was a pretty good one, but for some reason I was fairly certain it didn't work that way.

Poppa's answer was remarkably insightful and affected my perspective for the rest of my life. He said, "Because when God forgives you, He doesn't believe that you will ever sin again."

God believes in you.

God believes in your holiness. God believes in your purity. God believes in the work of His Son on the cross and in the resurrection. God does not look at us and think that we'll inevitably sin again. He knows that it's possible not to sin. Again, I'm not talking about Christian perfection or reaching a place where it's not possible for us to sin. I'm saying in any given situation at any given moment, it's possible to not sin. God expects us to walk there.

God speaks to us from this perspective of faith. He sees our hearts and intentions and can deal very harshly with the deliberately impure in heart, but for the sincere believer who is not trying to take advantage of the gospel, God has enormous, limitless hope. God believes in us and is an unshakable optimist when it comes to His church. One of the reasons He speaks to us at all is because He believes that we will respond and listen to His voice.

When we have a teacher, mentor, or parent who truly believes in us, we find it hard to let them down. We find ourselves working twice as hard in order to fulfill their expectations. This can become negative, subjecting us to severe pressure and a performance orientation, but it is healthy for us to respond to positive expectation with a motivated effort to fulfill the faith that has been placed in us. That external expectation makes us believe and understand what we are capable of. God's incredible expectation for our destiny, calling, and success should push us to excel. The prophetic expectation that hovers over our lives and speaks into our future should push us into greater things and remind us of the miracles that are possible in our calling and character. With God all things are possible. With God great things are expected.

In the Old Testament God dealt with people according to their sins. There was no remission of sins; there was only a covering. God looked at people's past history and current hearts and prophesied their sin and destruction. Yet even when God did this, people still turned from their sin in unexpected ways. Jonah prophesied to Ninevah, "Yet forty days and Ninevah shall be overthrown" (Jonah 3:4). There was no promise of forgiveness or restoration, yet the people of Ninevah repented with sackcloth, ashes, and fasting, and God had mercy on them.

Today God calls people out of their sin in an even more powerful way because there is now a lasting and eternal cleansing and removal of sins in the blood of His Son. There is so much more power available to live free. The Holy Spirit is available to empower us to live holy and walk with Him. When Jesus prophesied to Peter, "Before the rooster crows you will deny three times that you even know Me," (Mathew 26:34) He was looking at Peter's heart and knew that he did not have the capability to resist. The Shepherd would be struck, and the sheep would be scattered. Peter would not escape.

Now we have a way of escape prepared by God and enforced in our lives by the movement of the Holy Spirit. God looks at our hearts and knows that at any time His children can submit to the Holy Spirit and walk through temptation unscathed. Because of this, it is extremely rare that God would prophesy failure or sin into a believer's life. While I highly value letting the Holy Spirit say what He desires and not restraining Him with my theology, I would struggle with any prophecy telling a believer that they will inevitably fall into sin. God has great hopes for our holiness. Any believer who receives such a word should rise up in faith like Ninevah and preemptively repent and seek the Lord that such a thing does not happen.

I have an even stronger disagreement with any theology or doctrine of failure. Jesus died to save us from our sins, and Jesus is not a failure. Many have been trained to expect to sin every day, when Scripture teaches us the opposite. There are many factors that combine in this teaching: God's foreknowledge, our definition of sin, and our understanding of key passages like Romans chapter seven must all be considered. I can hardly lay out a holistic teaching on sanctification here, but I can invite you to hear God's voice of expectation removing the past and restoring a future of success and holiness. While we may make mistakes in the heat of the moment or struggle in our hearts, we can live above a deliberate (or in some translations "presumptuous") sin and choose holiness and purity.

Jesus said, "Most assuredly, I say to you, whoever commits sin is a slave of sin. And a slave does not abide in the house forever, but a son abides forever. Therefore if the Son makes you free, you shall be free indeed" (John 8:35-36). "Free indeed" is certainly a far cry from "we all sin every day."

Peter wrote, "but as He who called you is holy, you also be holy in all your conduct, because it is written, Be holy, for I am holy" (1 Peter 1:15). God is not frustrating us or teasing us with commands and standards we cannot meet in relationship with Him. We are empowered believers with God living on the inside of us. It is possible in God to be holy in all your conduct. In everything you do, you can be holy. You may not seem holy in everything you feel. You may not seem holy in every passing thought. You may not seem holy in every desire that pulls at you. But you can be holy in all you do. You can order every feeling, thought, and desire to bow to Jesus and walk in holiness.

The Bible says that we can do all things through Him who strengthens us (Philippians 4:13). It does not say we can do all things through Him who strengthens us except live free from sin.

An evangelist pointed out that Jesus said, "Most assuredly, I say to you, he who believes in Me, the works that I do he will do also; and greater works than these he will do, because I go to My Father," and one of the things Jesus did was go through every temptation and not sin. He said that we would do the same thing (John 14:12, Hebrews 4:15).

After healing a man in the temple, Jesus told him, "Sin no more, lest a worse thing come upon you" (John 5:14). He didn't say to "sin less" or "curb some bad habits" or suggest, "You'll probably keep sinning because you can't help it." Jesus expected people to repent and stop sinning. When Jesus says, "Sin no more," it is not only a command; it is an empowering prophetic word. He's saying what is possible and expected.

Jesus said the same to the woman caught in adultery, He refused to condemn her and then commanded and prophesied her holiness (John 8:11).

Paul wrote to the Romans, "What shall we say then? Shall we continue in sin that grace may abound? Certainly not!" (Romans 6:1). Paul said that we should "certainly not!" continue in sin. We are meant to leave sin behind; and that's not just some pious, religious phrase—it is a practical imperative. We must not continue in sin.

The apostle John stated, "My little children these things I write to you, so that you may not sin" (1 John

2:1a). His goal and purpose in writing, and the goal and purpose of all Scripture, is so you won't sin. God's word does not return void (Isaiah 55:1). There is real power in the Word of God to keep you from sin. John continued, "And if anyone sins, we have an Advocate with the Father, Jesus Christ the righteous" (1 John 2:1b). He wrote "if" anyone sins, not "when" anyone sins. Sin is not an inevitability, and any teaching that says conscious sin is inevitable and inescapable is error.

John went on to state, "Whoever abides in Him does not sin" (1 John 3:6). It is possible to stop sinning, and we do it by abiding and remaining in relationship with Jesus. We listen to His voice and continue to obey and respond to His voice and His word.

To those who were raised to believe that sin was inevitable, this may sound hard to believe, but Jesus said, "All things are possible to him who believes" (Mark 9:23). He did not add to that, "except living free from sin."

Whatever is not of faith is sin (Romans 14:23). The root of sin is unbelief, and the enemy desires to wreck your belief that you can live a holy life. Nevertheless, all of Scripture prophesies of a holy life for the children of God.

If it were according to your strength, ability, or holiness, it would be impossible; but what Jesus said about entering the kingdom is true of entering true holiness,: "With men this is impossible, but with God all things are possible" (Matthew 19:26).

God expects us to live out our salvation and live out our identities as sons of God. He believes that we will make it. He believes that we will be holy.

I have many stories of visions, dreams, and prophecies during the time period when I was struggling with pornography addiction. (Part of this may have to do with the dichotomy between holiness and God's gifts and callings, which I will explain in a later chapter.) Many of these dreams and visions came immediately within times of failure or right on the heels of repentance. God often used them to restore me, yet in most cases, I later fell into the same sin again. Still God chose to prophetically reveal Himself to me and to reveal my identity, my future, and my calling.

I used to rise at four in the morning to go to the office and pray. I was still struggling with pornography at this point, but I tried to develop a thriving prayer life. I walked around the church praying. An international evangelist had given a prophecy about Detroit and the Muslim population, and I would play it each morning during prayer. This morning I was struggling with hopelessness.

The overall ministry was a mess. I was physically, emotionally, and spiritually exhausted. I was sin-sick. I wanted to give up and quit. Previously in the year, I had watched a Muslim man who was an ESL student of mine die of cancer. I had prayed for his healing, realizing that with his limited English a supernatural encounter with the power of Jesus Christ was the only effective gospel demonstration he would ever have; but I did not have the faith or the understanding of how to pray. He died without Christ. It wrecked me.

A few months earlier, I had prayed for my neighbor, a believer, who was also battling cancer. She died too.

I grappled with these deaths each morning. I grappled with the fact that I wasn't leading anyone to Christ, that I was addicted to pornography, and that the ministry was spiraling out of control. I began to seriously cry out to God.

In the midst of my cries, God sent me a vision. I saw a mountain. It was huge and snowcapped, as big as Everest. Its peak was in the clouds, and around the center was wrapped a huge, red ribbon tied in a bow. The mountain was wrapped like a gift, and a name tag hung from the ribbon: "Jonathan."

> **Joshua 14:6-12 –** Then the children of Judah came to Joshua in Gilgal. And Caleb the son of Jephunneh the Kenizzite said to him: "You know the word which the LORD said to Moses the man of God concerning you and me in Kadesh Barnea. I was forty years old when Moses the servant of the LORD sent me from Kadesh Barnea to spy out the land, and I brought back word to him as it was in my heart. Nevertheless my brethren who went up with me made the heart of the people melt, but I wholly followed the LORD my God.
>
> "So Moses swore on that day, saying, 'Surely the land where your foot has trodden shall be your inheritance and your children's forever, because you have wholly followed the Lord my God.'
>
> "And now, behold, the LORD has kept me alive, as He said, these forty five years, ever since the LORD spoke this word to Moses while Israel wandered in the wilderness; and now, here I am this day, eighty-five years old. As yet I am as strong this day as on the day that Moses sent me; just as my strength was then, so now is

my strength for war, both for going out and for
coming in. Now therefore, give me this
mountain of which the Lord spoke in that day;
for you heard in that day how the Anakim were
there, and that the cities were great and
fortified. It may be that the LORD will be with
me, and I shall be able to drive them out as the
Lord said."

I had not been as faithful as Caleb had been, but like
Caleb, on the day of salvation, I allowed the Lord to take
my heart. I spoke in faith, "I'll do whatever You want me
to do," believing and expecting Him to enable me for the
task. I believed holiness was possible. I saw the enemies of
God and knew that with God, they could be defeated. Like
the children of Israel, I wandered in the wilderness of sin,
failing to enter the promise; but here God reminded me of
His future for me and His promise. "Give me this
mountain of which the Lord spoke in that day."

At the time I had the vision, I was still frustrated
and struggling in the wilderness, but the Lord had great
hopes and great expectations for me. Within one year, my
entire life had turned around. I was free from
pornography, and I was seeing people physically healed
and coming to the Lord through the ministry. God trusted
and believed in the vision He had for me, even more than
I did.

Prophecy inevitably speaks to potential. and is often
conditional.

There are times when God emphatically states what
He will do regardless of circumstances. There are times
when God responds to changing circumstances in order to
fulfill a prophetic word. God often moves heaven and

earth in order to fulfill what He has spoken. He does not break His word. God has exalted His word above His name. It will not come back to Him without result.

In the midst of God's unchanging and limitless faithfulness, prophecy is often conditional because God expects us to walk in right relationship with Him. He expects us to walk in faith-covenant. God does not prophesy our failure or our doom. He warns us in order to change our direction and cause us to repent, but as genuine believers, living by faith, God has no expectation that we will fail and so does not state a condition in every prophecy saying, "…but if you fall into unrepentant sin, none of this will come to pass…" In our Father's eyes, it's a given that we will walk in relationship with Him.

Israel was promised invincibility in battle, yet they soon lost because they violated their covenant and relationship with God (Joshua 1:5, Joshua 7:4). The priesthood was promised to never leave Eli's house, yet it did because of his sons' evil and sacrilegious lifestyle (1 Samuel 1-4). Israel was promised to enter the promise land, yet that generation died in the wilderness because of their unbelief (Deuteronomy 1). The list goes on and on. God made what sounded like an unconditional promise to an individual or a nation, yet He expected them to walk with Him in faith and obedience. The prophetic should give us assurance of our destiny but not apathy. Our relationship with God gives life to our calling and traction for the prophetic word to succeed.

God expects us to walk with Him, and the journey from prophecy to fulfillment is often unexpected. Joseph knew that his family would bow and that he would become a great ruler, but the journey led him into slavery and prison first. Prophecy gives us strength to stand under trial and test and is evidence of God's expectation of our success. God did not footnote Joseph's dreams with, "Fulfillment not guaranteed. The contents of this prophecy and its eventual fulfillment include severe testing and trial and may include slavery, false accusations of sexual assault, and many years in prison." God gave Joseph the word, expecting him to pass every test, and he did.

God speaks of "those things which do not exist as though they did" (Romans 4:17). God speaks prophetically into our lives before our calling and before our character or maturity are evident or even existent. God labeled Abraham "The Father of Many Nations" before he had a single child, expecting Abraham to be obedient. God spoke through Ananias to Saul about "the great things he must suffer for my name" when Saul had only been submitting to God for a few days.

Scripture is filled with examples of nameless men and women who became great because of the word God spoke over them. He spoke prophetically into each of these individuals' futures, believing that His word would make an impact on their lives and that their character and identity would be molded by this word. He saw the potential that they could not see. He believed that they would say "yes" to their destiny. He believed that they would endure great hardship and that they would remain faithful under severe trial. He believed that they would carry out supernatural exploits in His name by faith. He expected great things of them—greater even than they expected of themselves.

I absolutely believe that every one of these men and women could have said, "No." Each of them could have walked away from their destiny and backed off, but their stories are famous because they allowed God's enormous prophetic expectation to mold them into the people they were meant to be. God redeemed many of their mistakes along the way; but in the end, the prophetic word and revelation won out, and they became heroes of the faith. They vindicated God's incredible hope.

Some may struggle theologically with God giving me so many dreams and visions while I was still in my sin. The idea that God knows the future but expects us to live without sin is a theological knot. But I believe it is theologically sound that God believes in us and that He does not plan on our sin in the future. When I say, "I repent" from a pure heart, my sins are remitted, and I'm clean in His sight. He no longer expects me to sin. My sin is washed away. It is removed as far as the east is from the west. He remembers it no more, and He treats me as a Son. Even though I have the potential to sin again, I am forgiven, and it is possible for me to be free. God views me through that possibility.

God believes in us. God believes in you. God has a mountain for you—a place of inheritance and success, a battlefield for you to conquer, an enemy for you to destroy, a promised land for you to grasp. Leave the wilderness, and take the place of promise. God believes you will make it.

ACTION STEP

Ask God:

Lord, do You believe in me?

Say Aloud:

I am dead to sin and alive to God. I consider myself dead to sin. (Romans 6:11)

Sin shall not have dominion over me. I am not under the law. I am under grace. (Romans 6:14)

I abide in Jesus. I'm not going to sin. (1 John 3:6)

I am not condemned. I am forgiven. I am free to go and sin no more. (John 8:11)

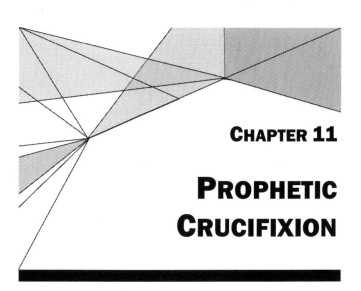

CHAPTER 11

PROPHETIC CRUCIFIXION

With my hands spread out above me, I worshiped God, singing the song "Here I am to Worship" as loudly as I could, when suddenly the Holy Spirit overwhelmed me with a vision: My arms were spread wide, and I was hanging from a cross. My body hung slack. It was me—my body—naked, bruised, bloody and almost unrecognizable. I was gasping for breath. My hands were pierced. My feet had nails in them. My side had a tear in it. My chest heaved up and down as I suffocated. Blood poured from my wounds. My body was tattooed from head to toe with writing. Each word described my sin. Across my forehead was the word "lust." "Pornography" was written across my chest. "Abusive" was on my abdomen. My skin was covered in the stain of sin. I gasped for breath. I died.

The picture was shocking, and to some degree it still is. But I rejoice in it. I died with Christ, and now I am free from myself—free to live for Him.

At the heart of sanctification is the cross and the work of Jesus Christ, and it is a finished work. We are in the process of walking out what Christ did two-thousand years ago on the cross, and the power of the cross and resurrection flows through our lives, producing a resurrected life.

> **Romans 6:2-4 –** How shall we who died to sin live any longer in it? Or do you not know that as many of us as were baptized into Christ Jesus were baptized into His death? Therefore we were buried with Him through baptism into death, that just as Christ was raised from the dead by the glory of the Father, even so we also should walk in newness of life.

Your old nature, who you were before Jesus, who you were in sin, who you were in the natural—your "sin nature"—is dead.

It's dead.

It's confirmed-dead. It has no pulse. It has no life. It was crucified. Your "old man" was crucified. Nails went through your hands. Nails went through your feet. A spear went in your side. Your brow was pierced with thorns. Your blood ran out. You suffocated. You were buried in a tomb and a stone was rolled over the tomb. It was sealed. You are not getting out. You are dead. You have a headstone recording your death: "Dead in Christ: 33 A.D." There is no possibility of that person coming back to life.

> **Romans 6:6-7 –** ...our old man was crucified with Him, that the body of sin might be done away with, that we should no longer be slaves of

sin. For he who has died has been freed from
sin.

Your death is a past tense event. We wake up every morning and leave our old man in the grave, living out of the revelation of Christ within. Your old man was crucified with Jesus, and this means that the "body of sin" was "done away with." The whole bundle of sin, sinful desires, and sinful motivations is gone, removed, nailed, killed, and buried with Christ in the grave. It is never coming back. Don't ever visit it. Don't carry it with you. It's gone. You aren't chained to it anymore. You aren't a slave to yourself anymore. You have been set free from you because you have died, and "he who has died has been freed from sin."

Now we are ordered to "reckon yourselves to be dead indeed to sin but alive to God in Christ Jesus our Lord" (Romans 6:11). We are ordered to reckon, or consider, or account, ourselves dead to sin. We are supposed to genuinely believe that we are dead to sin. We are to know and make a mathematical, logical calculation that we are really dead to sin. Not just dead to sin, but dead indeed to sin. Really dead. Actually dead.

We are not just free. We are free indeed. Really free! We are dead to ourselves and alive to God in Christ Jesus. We live to Him in Jesus. It is wrong to wake up in the morning and say, "I hope I can make it through the day without sinning." We are to spring out of bed knowing that we will be free because free is who we are. Free is what Christ has done for us. The one who sinned is dead. The One who doesn't sin is alive (Galatians 2:20). This is the truth of God's Word, and we must agree with it. This is what the Spirit says to us every day—if we are willing to listen.

> **Colossians 2:11-13 –** In Him you were also circumcised with the circumcision made without hands, by putting off the body of the sins of the flesh, by the circumcision of Christ, buried with Him in baptism, in which you also were raised with Him through faith in the working of God, who raised Him from the dead. And you, being dead in your trespasses and the uncircumcision of your flesh, He has made alive together with Him, having forgiven you all trespasses.

Our flesh—our sin-nature—was cut off by the cross. It has been removed. We are meant to "put off" the old man. It is dead, and now we take that dead body, that dead memory, and cast it off. We don't keep the old man's things in our house. We don't keep the old man's habits. We don't talk the way the old man did. We don't behave the way the old man did. Because he is dead. The new man is alive—happy, living, and brand new in Christ. We are forgiven, redeemed, restored, reborn, and set free.

> **Romans 6:10 –** For the death that He died, He died to sin once for all; but the life that He lives, He lives to God.

Jesus died once for all. He doesn't have to die again for you. You were killed when He was killed (2 Corinthians 5:14). If you have to go to the cross every day, then so does Jesus. But Jesus died "once for all." Sin was dealt with. You were dealt with. You were executed for your sinful ways when Christ was crucified. He who knew no sin became sin for us (2 Corinthians 5:21). That means our ways died on the cross just as our deeds did. The Spirit is speaking now, urging us to forget what went before and press on into the "new man" who lives out the ways and deeds of Christ.

> **Colossians 3:1-3 –** If then you were raised with Christ, seek those things which are above, where Christ is, sitting at the right hand of God. Set your mind on things above, not on things on the earth. For you died, and your life is hidden with Christ in God.

We have been resurrected in Christ as a new creation and a new man and now we seek the things above. We seek Christ. We set our minds on Him.

We see Him in His glory, and as we behold His glory we become like Him. "When we see Him, we shall be like Him for we will see Him as He is" (1 John 3:2). We set our minds on things above. We consider ourselves dead to sin and put our minds in the heavens because we died.

To discover who we are, we have to look at Jesus. "For you died…" you can't find yourself in what went on before. That person is sealed in a tomb, absolutely dead. You can't look at him anymore. "Your life is hidden with Christ in God." You have to search yourself out in Christ Himself. You are in Him. The Spirit leads us into this discovery and revelation—a discovery of ourselves in Christ.

When God looks at you and when the enemy looks at you, there is little to distinguish between you and Jesus because of what Christ has done and because you are hidden in Him. This is the great mystery of righteousness.

We know that somewhere between this earth and heaven, our immaturities are evident since the Spirit and the enemy can both relate to us according to them. Nevertheless, God's throne is where our minds are meant to be. We fix our eyes on Jesus. As we fix our eyes on Him, we see ourselves in Him.

> **Galatians 2:20 –** I have been crucified with Christ; it is no longer I who live, but Christ lives in me; and the life which I now live in the flesh I live by faith in the Son of God, who loved me and gave Himself for me.

Paul's statement is true of all believers. We all have been crucified with Christ. You have been crucified with Christ. You don't live anymore. Christ lives in you. You live out the life of Christ in your body by faith. By knowing and believing who you are in Him, dead to sin and alive to God, you obtain by faith not only the righteousness of Christ in the spiritual, but you walk it out in the natural. Righteousness becomes practical. It becomes holiness and a holy life.

> **Ephesians 4:22-24 –** ...put off, concerning your former conduct, the old man which grows corrupt according to the deceitful lusts, and be renewed in the spirit of your mind, and that you put on the new man which was created according to God, in true righteousness and holiness.

By faith we renew our mind to this truth, and we forsake our old ways and old character because these have been killed. We put on the new man. By faith we put on a new identity, created by God in true righteousness and holiness. The identity we have now is truly righteous and truly holy. It's not some halfway, in between, not-quite-there-yet identity. It's the identity of Christ. He's perfect.

> **John 6:63 –** It is the Spirit who gives life; the flesh profits nothing. The words that I speak to you are spirit, and they are life.

These words of the Holy Spirit are what give life. They are the words of Jesus. Put them in your heart and your mind, and walk out your new identity.

> **1 Peter 1:1-4 –** Grace and peace be multiplied to you in the knowledge of God and of Jesus our Lord, as His divine power has given to us all things that pertain to life and godliness, through the knowledge of Him who called us by glory and virtue, by which have been given to us exceedingly great and precious promises, that through these you may be partakers of the divine nature, having escaped the corruption that is in the world through lust.

Through the divine power of God, we have everything we need for life and for godliness. That means everything we need to presently live a holy and godly life is provided by supernatural resurrection-power. Through the knowledge of Christ, we have promises that give us holiness. We partake of the divine nature. We don't live as empty slates. We put off the old man and drink in the new man, who is alive in Christ.

> **Colossians 3:8-10a –** But now you yourselves are to put off all these: anger, wrath, malice, blasphemy, filthy language out of your mouth. Do not lie to one another, since you have put off the old man with his deeds, and have put on the new man who is renewed in knowledge according to the image of Him who created him...

We throw away evil behavior and motivations, not by punishing ourselves or conditioning ourselves, but by repenting and believing that we are dead. The dead don't become angry. Dead people don't have wrath or malice any more. They cannot blaspheme or use filthy language. They cannot lie. They're dead. We simply throw the corpse off our minds and hearts and put on Jesus inside. We become new according to the knowledge of who we are in Him and what we really look like.

> **1 Corinthians 5:17 –** Therefore, if anyone is in Christ, he is a new creation; old things have passed away; behold, all things have become new.

We still experience temptation. We still have habits and memories from a life of sin and from who we were before, but we are learning and growing in our new selves. We are free to be someone new—finally and forever. Anyone, anywhere, at any time in Christ is a new creation. Whether you gave your life to Christ yesterday or fifty years ago, the power of the Cross cuts off every obligation to sinful identity and sinful behavior. We are now free to choose holiness and to choose life.

At one time we walked in ignorance and helplessness against our sinful desires. We were bound to them and unable to be free or even to say "no." We might have exercised our natural willpower or self-control, but our sinful identity was guaranteed to assert itself. Full freedom was not a choice, and we were defined by our sin. We were sinners.

Now we stand before God as saints, holy and acceptable before Him. We partake of the divine nature and have stopped partaking of our sinful nature because we have been cut off from it. It is dead and buried. We can dig it up if we want to. But we are free to leave it in the ground and live in the newness of resurrection life.

Now we live in a process of growing up into all the things that God has for us in Jesus. We are learning about ourselves in Christ, and this is a walk of faith. There is no getting to the bottom of the wonders of what it means to be dead in Christ and alive as sons of God. Our memories and humanity tell us that we are still who we used to be. Our bodies still feel the same. We may still have old cravings, habits, and temptations. But we are not those things. We are defined by life in Christ.

God commands us to consider ourselves dead to sin. When we believe sin is an inevitability, we disobey this command. We must seize God's truth and promise by faith and live it out day by day. You have been nailed to the cross with all your sin; and now, today, you are a new creation—free from all you have been. You are free to be all you are meant to be in Christ.

ACTION STEP

Ask God:

Show me what it means to be crucified with Christ.

Lord, is there anything from my old life and old man with which I still identify?

Lord, show me what is dead and what is alive in me.

Say Aloud:

I was crucified with Christ. My hands were pinned to the cross. My feet were pinned to the cross. My sin and sinful nature are buried in the grave. I live a new life by faith in the Son of God.

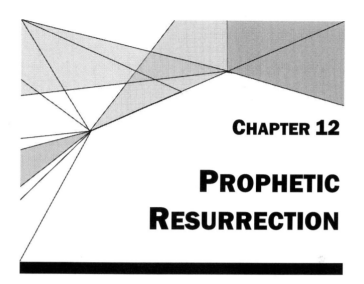

CHAPTER 12

PROPHETIC RESURRECTION

My friend Robert committed a high-profile crime several years ago. The crime he committed brought stigma with it. His face and name were on the news. He was identified with his sin. He had to restructure his life. He grieved and repented of his sin, and he took drastic steps to avoid doing anything like it again. He went through a restoration process with multiple churches. He repented. He loves Jesus.

While he and I are not the closest friends, his friendship has meant a lot to me. Robert is a constant reminder of God's grace and restoration. My sins have never been uncovered the same way his were. My sins are not a permanent stigma giving me a criminal record or a reputation in my community.

But my sins were just as sinful.

One morning I was worshipping next to Robert in a church building. We had our hands raised and were belting a song about grace. My eyes were closed, and I was overwhelmed with the mercy and grace of God. I could hear Robert's voice beside me. I went into a vision: Robert and I stood before the throne of God. Jesus was there. His eyes were like fire, and a crown sat on His head. I looked over and was nearly blinded by the brightness of Robert's robe. It shone white. There wasn't a single spot or wrinkle. I looked down at my own robe, and it shone with the same brightness.

You are the righteousness of God.

Robert and I were back in a church building, eyes closed, hands raised, singing to the God who had redeemed us from every vile thing and pronounced us clean in His sight. Tears rolled down my face. I couldn't sing loud enough.

NEW CREATIONS

2 Corinthians 5:17-21 – Therefore, if anyone is in Christ, he is a new creation; old things have passed away; behold, all things have become new. Now all things are of God, who has reconciled us to Himself through Jesus Christ and has given us the ministry of reconciliation, that is, that God was in Christ reconciling the world to Himself, not imputing their trespasses to them, and has committed to us the word of reconciliation.

Now then, we are ambassadors for Christ, as though God were pleading through us: we implore you on Christ's behalf, be reconciled to God. For He made Him who knew no sin to be sin for us, that we might become the righteousness of God in Him.

We live in newness of resurrection life. We have been reborn in the resurrection of Christ, and all that we knew of ourselves before must be exchanged for knowing ourselves as new creations. Regardless of how we feel, God identifies us as new creations. We must submit to His truth.

We live in intimacy with God through Jesus Christ, and God has entrusted us to call the rest of the world into that intimacy. God does not hold our sins against us. He does not hold the world's sins against them. He calls them to Himself. Now we live to call the world into intimacy with God through Jesus Christ.

We were raised from the dead as new creations in Christ, but our old memories remain. Our minds have been touched and flooded with the grace of God, but we have the freedom to choose where to live and think.

Our spirits have been made new, but our bodies remain the same. When we were born again, and raised from death, it occurred on the inside. It wasn't a physical renewal of our bodies—that will happen at the resurrection at the end of time (1 Corinthians 15). Our bodies can still have wrong desires, and our minds still have the ability to drift from the newness of life we have been given. If we set our minds and our wills on pleasing sinful desires, we are living in death, not in resurrection life.

We have a Helper and a Comforter. We are empowered by the indwelling life of Christ. We were raised from the dead when the Holy Spirit sprung up within us, joining our Spirit (1 Corinthians 6:17) and bringing new life and new freedom. Our bodies still have sinful desires, but the Spirit within us lives to fulfill Christ's desires. We don't have to live based on the desires of our bodies or minds, but we can choose to make our life-choices based on the will and mind of Christ.

This new identity is not achieved. God has already done it. You don't accomplish it. It is already accomplished. God did it through Christ.

We receive this identity by grace through faith. We believe that what the Scripture says about our position is true and that faith transforms our behavior. We receive grace. We conform to the truth we believe.

This chapter is not about actions to achieve your identity. It is not about doing. I hope the rest of the book gives you highly practical action steps, but this chapter is about what God has done apart from your effort.

Transformation occurs when we believe. There is wide variation in how one's faith in their identity takes practical action, but there is no action you can take to make yourself a new creation. The revelation in these Scriptures was given to struggling Christians. It revealed that God had already made them new creations. The writers applied the truth of what God had done to these struggling believers.

Do You Not Know?

The phrase "do you not know?" appears throughout the Epistles. The phrase suggests disbelief on the part of the writer and often introduces an emphatic declaration that if the readers did know the truth about themselves, their character and behavior would change. A declaration about who we are in Christ almost always follows the phrase "do you not know." The core of transformation after new birth is the revelation of how the gospel and the Spirit continue to speak of who we are.

Paul challenged the notion of continuing in sin by telling the story of how the gospel has changed our identity. He opened this story with the phrase "do you not know."

What shall we say then? Shall we continue in sin that grace may abound? Certainly not! How shall we who died to sin live any longer in it? Or do you not know that as many of us as were baptized into Christ Jesus were baptized into His death? (Romans 6:1-3)

If we continue in sin, we do not really know and understand that we have truly died to sin. Paul's statement implies that they would not have this thought or behavior if they knew that they were baptized or immersed into Christ Jesus and that they were baptized or immersed into Christ's death. Paul went on to explain this immersion and new life in Christ, telling his story through the Greek word for the English preposition "with." In the final verse, the Greek word for "with" is part of another word which is translated into English as "conformed" (Ton, p. 169):

> ➢ . . . We have been united with Him in his death, we will also be raised to life as He was. (Romans 6:5 NLT)
> ➢ We know that our old sinful selves were crucified with Christ so that sin might lose its power in our lives . . . (Romans 6:6 NLT)
> ➢ . . . we died with Christ . . . (Romans 6:8 NLT)
> ➢ For we died and were buried with Christ by baptism. (Romans 6:4a NLT)

➤ . . . we shall also live with Him (Romans 6:8 NLT)

➤ . . . together with Christ we are heirs of God's glory . . . (Romans 8:17 NLT)

➤ . . . if we indeed suffer with Him . . . (Romans 8:17)

➤ That we also may be glorified with Him (Romans 8:17 NASB)

➤ . . . to become conformed to the image of His Son . . . (Romans 8:29)

Each of these verses identifies us "with" Christ in what He has done to redeem and transform humanity. God has united us with Christ. What identifies Christ— His perfect relationship with the Father, His character, His power, His suffering, His self-sacrifice, His resurrection life—now identifies us.

Paul asked the Corinthians, "Do you not know that you are the temple of God and that the Spirit of God dwells in you?" (1 Corinthians 3:16). We are vessels for God's life. We are containers for His Spirit. We are one spirit with Him, and His life is united with ours. The way we treat our bodies and souls changes when we know that we are temples for the Spirit of God. This so identifies the Christian life that when Paul told the Corinthians to examine themselves, he asked if they really knew that Christ lived within them:

2 Corinthians 13:5 – Examine yourselves as to whether you are in the faith. Test yourselves. Do you not know yourselves, that Jesus Christ is in you?—unless indeed you are disqualified.

The life of Christ on the inside of us works itself out in our lives, demonstrating that we are in the faith. Paul both challenged and informed the Corinthians. He encouraged them by instructing them in who they really are. He challenged them to throw away old mindsets and lower standards. He opened up the wonder of what Christ has made us. He reminded them that they were now empowered by the life of God within. He challenged them to examine whether their faith had accessed that life and whether their behavior corresponded.

God's finished work has made us one with Christ, but we collaborate and live in partnership with God's work and truth. After Romans 6:3 Paul's next "do you not know" statement is in verse 16:

> **Romans 6:16-19 –** Do you not know that to whom you present yourselves slaves to obey, you are that one's slaves whom you obey, whether of sin leading to death, or of obedience leading to righteousness? But God be thanked that though you were slaves of sin, yet you obeyed from the heart that form of doctrine to which you were delivered. And having been set free from sin, you became slaves of righteousness. I speak in human terms because of the weakness of your flesh. For just as you presented your members as slaves of uncleanness, and of lawlessness leading to more lawlessness, so now present your members as slaves of righteousness for holiness.

Paul lacked confidence in his reader's ability to hear and take his words seriously, so he radicalized his communication about obedience. He told His readers that they are slaves. Their master was the one to whom they had given themselves. Whoever they obeyed ruled their lives—either sin or righteousness. Freedom from sin means slavery to righteousness. We are bound to righteousness. We are restricted to righteousness. Righteousness is our work and our identity. Righteousness masters our actions, and we have been made the very righteousness of God.

RAISED TO THE THRONE

Ephesians 1:15-23 – Therefore I also, after I heard of your faith in the Lord Jesus and your love for all the saints, do not cease to give thanks for you, making mention of you in my prayers: that the God of our Lord Jesus Christ, the Father of glory, may give to you the spirit of wisdom and revelation in the knowledge of Him, the eyes of your understanding being enlightened; that you may know what is the hope of His calling, what are the riches of the glory of His inheritance in the saints, and what is the exceeding greatness of His power toward us who believe, according to the working of His mighty power which He worked in Christ when He raised Him from the dead and seated Him at His right hand in the heavenly places, far above all principality and power and might and dominion, and every name that is named, not only in this age but also in that which is to come.

And He put all things under His feet, and

gave Him to be head over all things to the
church, which is His body, the fullness of Him
who fills all in all.

Paul prayed that the Ephesian church would have
both personal and corporate revelation. Paul could
prophesy and write Scripture, but he couldn't make them
receive it. They needed to have a personal revelation of
this truth of God.

He wanted them to understand the hope that they
had in God's calling. He wanted them to understand the
riches of their inheritance as holy ones. Paul asked God to
give them revelation of all the things they gained by being
in Christ. "Riches of the glory of His inheritance" means a
wealth of glory in God's provision and treasure as well as
the empowerment that comes from being a child of God.
Paul also wanted them to understand the immense power
of God "toward us." God's power is toward you. It is for
you. It works on your behalf. Immense and immeasurable
ability flows from the throne of God to you.

> **Ephesians 2:1-6 –** And you He made alive, who
> were dead in trespasses and sins, in which you
> once walked according to the course of this
> world, according to the prince of the power of
> the air, the spirit who now works in the sons of
> disobedience, among whom also we all once
> conducted ourselves in the lusts of our flesh,
> fulfilling the desires of the flesh and of the mind,
> and were by nature children of wrath, just as
> the others.
>
> But God, who is rich in mercy, because of
> His great love with which He loved us, even

> when we were dead in trespasses, made us alive
> together with Christ (by grace you have been
> saved), and raised us up together, and made us
> sit together in the heavenly places in Christ
> Jesus, that in the ages to come He might show
> the exceeding riches of His grace in His kindness
> toward us in Christ Jesus.

God raised you with and in Christ. This resurrection marked the start of a new life. You once lived under the influence and control of the world, the flesh, and the devil. You once were under the wrath and condemnation of God. Now you live under the influence, control, and reign of God. You are now hidden in Christ, living within His approval and righteousness.

God's Spirit breathed new life into you, and now you have conquered through and with Christ Jesus. Not only have you been raised from the dead, but you have been raised to sit where Christ sits in heavenly places. You live where Christ lives.

Christ lives in us, yet Christ also sits at the right hand of the Father. We sit with Christ, yet our spirits are also within our bodies here on earth. This describes our spiritual position in Christ. You have been given a seat of authority and power.

Your position is in Christ. You have your life in Him, and His position is now your position. We live from a place of authority. We live from a place of acceptance. We live from a place of power. God says that you have been "accepted in the Beloved" (Ephesians 1:6). You live in the love that God has for His Son. You live in the pleasure that God has in Jesus. You live in the approval and victory of Christ.

We receive this approval and victory by grace through faith. We believe that God forgives us and approves of us as His children. We believe that we have victory over sin, the flesh, and the devil. As we open our eyes wider and wider to this revelation, our thoughts and emotions come into line with our place in Christ.

RAISED IN POWER

Most of the issues and struggles Christians face are power issues. There is something that has power over them. It could be an addiction. It could be depression. It could be anxiety or worry. Regardless of the issue, Christ has made us more powerful than any affliction, oppression, or bondage. We were born into resurrection life by resurrection power, and we were not born as weaklings but as mighty men and women of God. We were born into an army designed to manifest and demonstrate Christ, destroying all the work of the enemy (Romans 8; 1 John 3:8).

> **John 8:36** – Therefore if the son makes you free you shall be free indeed.

We were born into freedom. Free is not just an option; it's not just available; it's part of who we are. We are free; and if we are not living free, it's because we have been deceived.

We are not victims of sin. We are not weak and powerless against it. We sin because we choose it. We have the power and ability to break free and live in dominion over it. We can make a different choice.

Romans 6:14 – For sin shall not have dominion over you, for you are not under law but under grace.

1 Corinthians 6:12 – All things are lawful for me, but all things are not helpful. All things are lawful for me, but I will not be brought under the power of any.

Paul refused to be brought under the power of anything. He knew that in Christ he had the power to overcome any enslaving force. Freedom was a choice, and he refused anything but absolute freedom. He had the will, the desire, and the power to refuse any master but Christ.

Romans 5:17 – For if by the one man's offense death reigned through the one, much more those who receive abundance of grace and of the gift of righteousness will reign in life through the One, Jesus Christ.

Where sin and death once reigned, we reign. We reign. We rule over sin. We rule over the effects of the fall of humanity. We destroy the works of the devil. We live holy lives. We set captives free. We cast out demons. We heal the sick. We raise the dead. Grace and righteousness have made us kings and lords under the King of kings and the Lord of lords. We reign in Jesus Christ.

We are seated with Christ at the center of power— the right hand of God's throne. Christ's body is seated on the throne high above all spiritual power. His body extends to the earth through us. We reign in this life.

Galatians 5:1 – Stand fast therefore in the liberty by which Christ has made us free and do not be entangled again with a yoke of bondage.

We were born free. We must stand fast in our identity as free sons of God. We live in liberty and refuse to be entangled with any yoke.

Paul wrote this as a practical command, not as wishful thinking. Freedom is real, available, and practical. He wrote this to a church bound by legalism, but he did not write to them as weak, pitiful, and bound. He wrote to them as free sons and daughters. He told them to reject that yoke because they had the power and ability to do so.

For the Galatians, this meant refusing to be told they weren't righteous because they didn't keep the Old Testament law. Working for their righteousness was the yoke that was entangling them. Rather than feeling justified through their own good works, they were to live in freedom from condemnation and from a guilty conscience because of the free gift of righteousness. They said "no" to guilt and shame. They said, "no" to the compulsion to try to earn righteousness.

For me, this means refusing the temptations of pornography. I have been set free. I am righteous. I am not a pornography-addict. That sin doesn't stain me or identify me. When temptation comes, I know and say these things. I stand fast in my freedom. I identify pornography as a yoke of bondage. I identify myself as free and righteous. Giving in to that temptation is not consistent with who I am. I draw strength from what God has done. I stand fast in the freedom He has given me.

> **2 Corinthians 5:21 –** For He made Him who knew no sin to be sin for us, that we might become the righteousness of God in Him.

Our identity is righteousness. When God looks at us walking in the blood of Christ and the power of the Spirit, He sees us as righteous. The angels and Satan look at us walking in the blood of Christ and the power of the Spirit and see us shining with God's righteousness. In Christ, we are right with God. That's not just our condition; it's actually who we are. We are the righteousness of God. We must choose to walk in who we are and refuse to violate that identity.

> **Hebrews 10:14 –** By one sacrifice He has perfected forever those who are being made holy.

Through the one-time sacrifice of Christ Jesus, God completed our identities. We were raised with Christ as new men and women. Our identity in Christ is perfect and true, and when we walk that out, we manifest holiness. The completed, perfected identity we have in Him is being practically revealed in our lives. It is already a finished work. Our lives are in the process of conforming to that work's perfection. We are in the process of living out what God has already completed in the spiritual realm and in our own spirits.

Growth is our lives catching up to the heavenly reality. "Out of His fullness we have all received grace in place of grace already given." (John 1:16, NIV). We have access to the fullness of the power and life of Christ. We receive grace—God's gift of empowerment.

Hebrews 10:14 does not mean that we walk around completely perfect and unable to sin. We walk as redeemed men and women who are spiritually complete. We guard our spirits from defilement, with submitted souls, ruling over our bodies (2 Corinthians 7:1).

> **Ephesians 4:24 –** And that you put on the new man which was created according to God in true righteousness and holiness.

We put on this new man by faith. We believe what God says about us, and we behave accordingly. We say "no" to the desires of our flesh and "yes" to the desires of our spirit. We identify everything that a son of God would not do, pin it to the cross, and run toward Jesus.

KNOWN BY THE SPIRIT

> **1 Corinthians 2:12 –** Now we have received, not the spirit of the world, but the Spirit who is from God, that we might know the things that have been freely given to us by God.

The Holy Spirit reveals the truth of who we are and what God has done for us. His revelation is free. We must listen and receive. We know these things by the Spirit. The Spirit confirms them and reminds us of them (John 14:26). As we walk with the Spirit, He continually reveals our lives of intimacy and empowerment. By the Spirit we look at Jesus and realize that we are not far from Him. We are seated with Him at the right hand of God.

The Gospel is the story of our transformation

through Christ's sacrifice and love. Two thousand years ago, God completed a work in Christ. He included us in that work. We were there when Christ was crucified. We were there when Christ was raised. We are in Heaven now, sitting with Christ on His throne. God wants us to see this. Jesus was beaten until He was unrecognizable so that we could finally see who we really are in Him.

> **Proverbs 27:3 –** As a man thinks in his heart so is he.

> **Colossians 2:6 –** Therefore, as you received Christ Jesus the Lord, so walk in Him.

As we receive revelation of who we are in Christ, we act out of who we are in Christ. We walk in Him. We live day-to-day in His character and power. We know that Christ does not fly into fits of rage; we don't either. We know that Christ healed all who came to Him; we too pray for the sick. The more we identify with Christ's life within, the more we live and act like Jesus. This includes both Christ-like character and Christ-like power in ministry (John 14:12, Mark 16:7-18). Christ's life is available to us through relationship with Him and because of what God has done.

The circumstances of our lives and our ever-fading stumblings lose their power to label us. We find firmer and firmer footing on the foundation of Christ. We receive the truth about who we are by grace through faith. We believe it beyond what our past tells us and beyond how we feel. We live out of the knowledge of who we are in Christ rather than who we have been or what we have done. We live in a process of renewing our minds to this truth through hearing the revelation of the Spirit.

The desires of the flesh lose their grip on us because they are a distant echo of pleasure or satisfaction compared to the voice of truth and the Spirit inside us. We "hold true to what we have attained" (Philippians 3:16). Our lives conform to spiritual reality. Our righteousness creates a bold security in who we are.

We become bold as lions (Proverbs 28:1). We say with Nehemiah, "Should such a man as I run away? . . ." (Nehemiah 6:11). Should such a man as I lust? Should such a woman as I hold onto bitterness? Should such a person as I lie? Steal? Covet?

How can you? You are the righteousness of God in Christ. Those things are dead to you, and you are dead to them. You are alive to Christ and hidden in Him. You are free to live His life today.

ACTION STEP

Ask God:

Who am I to You?

Who am I in You?

Say Aloud:

I am a new creation.
I am reconciled to God.
God doesn't count my past sins against me.
I am an ambassador for Christ.
God's power is for me and toward me.
I have been raised with Christ.
I am seated with Christ in heavenly places.
The Son has set me free. I am really free. I am free indeed.
I will reign in life through Jesus Christ.

> I will reign over sin
>
> I will reign over my desires
>
> I will reign over my emotions
>
> I will reign over my thoughts

I am complete in Christ. I am being made holy. I will live
a holy life in Christ Jesus.

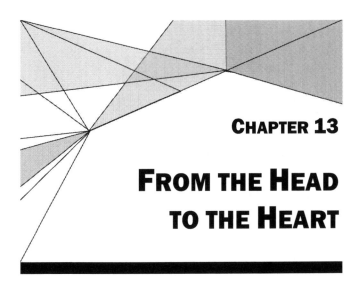

CHAPTER 13

FROM THE HEAD TO THE HEART

I told my friend Marco that he had to do whatever it took to quit heroin, or he would die. I had picked him up from the hospital because he had an infection in his foot. The hospital treated him and released him as quickly as possible.

Marco had been addicted to heroin for several years. At one point he had been clean for a year and half, and then went back to his old ways. I loved Marco, and I had given him a place to sleep several times, cleaning up after him and trying to help him in whatever ways I could. Sometimes I probably gave him too much grace, but he was fairly honest with me, which was refreshing. Marco came from a Catholic background, and we did impromptu Bible studies together often. His life was such a mess that he rarely followed through on what he learned, but he liked to hear and listen.

Over the summer Marco had been declining steadily. His body was covered in sores because withdrawal symptoms made him itch and scratch holes in his skin. I could tell he was about to hit bottom. I told him, "If you continue doing this, you're going to die."

"You think I don't know this?" he said. I could hear the frustration in his voice. "You think I want to live this way? Nobody does." He talked about the kind of life he wanted and about what he had when he was clean. "I had all those things. But I still wanted heroin. I found something that made me feel good. How do you change what you want? How do you change your heart?"

It is one of the best questions I have ever been asked.

For Marco, the gospel was the answer to changing his heart. A few months later, we sat in my car in the middle of the night, and I shared my testimony with him for what must have been the tenth time.

He looked at me and said, "I want that."

I walked him through the gospel and surrendering his life to Jesus.

He prayed, "Hello, God . . . it's Marco . . . uh . . . it's an emergency."

I think it is still one of the best prayers I have ever heard. After he prayed, I put my hand on his shoulder and prayed for him. As I prayed, he passed out in the seat next to me. I wasn't sure what to do, so I just kept praying for him. He came awake a few minutes later and wasn't sure what had happened. I told him not to worry about it. One month later he was picked up by the police for something small and finished his detox in prison. When he was released, a friend and I started discipling him, and he's still clean today.

Marco's story isn't a perfect example of a changed

heart. He and I don't talk much anymore. After he found his footing, he decided to go back to the Catholic Church. He wanted to live a nice life as a "good Catholic." I know that God has more for Marco than that.

Even though Marco's story is far from perfect, his question in the car comes back to me again and again. It's a question I've asked myself so many times, and it's a question that has many answers. Hearing it in Marco's emotion-strained voice never left me. He knew his life was at stake. The question mattered to him.

Many of us know truths about ourselves and about the Christian life, but there remains a distance between that knowledge in our heads and its true presence in our hearts. Many of us are even aware of this.

Marco knew the gospel. He had heard it many times. He knew that heroin would kill him and that today's high wasn't worth tomorrow. There was a disconnect between that knowledge and any heart-level motivation.

I know many people who intellectually understand their identity in Christ. They have been taught it over and over. Some of them teach it themselves. They know the verses and the teaching. They've even had experiences with the Holy Spirit revealing these things. Yet their lives are a mess. They have the knowledge in their head. They know it well enough to teach a series, but their hearts remain untouched.

Many more of us experience great victory in some parts of our lives but struggle to gain a grasp of the gospel in specific areas of life. We know who we are in Christ and live in victory over numerous issues, yet we may still grapple with one specific area. We struggle to really see and realize and understand who we are when it comes to anxiety, lust, bitterness, or relationships (especially romantic ones). We have the right information, but part of the heart still needs to be touched and transformed. We still seem to lack faith in certain areas.

How does the truth move from our head to our heart?

I found another answer to Marco's question in sharing the gospel with another young man, Khalid. Khalid came from a restricted Muslim nation and practiced Islam. Though his English was fairly good, he wanted me to help him improve so that he could get his GED. I told him my testimony, including the gospel and the message of the cross, and explained that because of what God had done in my life, I wanted to help others. I told him that I wanted to help him learn English and find a better job but that I especially wanted to help him learn how to be close to God. I told him that I would use stories from the Bible to teach him English and how to be close to God at the same time. He agreed.

During our thirty-eighth Bible study, Khalid gave his life to Christ. He confessed his faith that Jesus died on the cross for his sins and that Jesus rose from the dead. He confessed that Jesus was his King and Master and that he would do whatever Jesus commanded.

When I went home that day, I worshipped God. I had shared the gospel with Khalid again and again. I had done Bible study after Bible study explaining God's plan of salvation from creation to Christ. I had prayed with tears many times asking God to save Khalid. Now that it had happened, I was shocked.

How did this happen? It seemed like such a miracle. There was no fiery gospel message. There was no altar call.

There was no tangible presence of God. Khalid didn't have a dream or a vision. He wasn't healed. I didn't have a prophetic word or a word of knowledge for him. Somehow, at some point, in the midst of those Bible studies, the Holy Spirit grabbed hold of Khalid's heart, and he experienced Jesus as a real Person.

> **Mark 4:26-29 –** And He said, "The kingdom of God is as if a man should scatter seed on the ground. He sleeps and rises night and day, and the seed sprouts and grows; he knows not how. The earth produces by itself, first the blade, then the ear, then the full grain in the ear. But when the grain is ripe, at once he puts in the sickle, because the harvest has come."

Jesus taught that the kingdom works like a farmer who scatters seed. He scatters the seed, but he can't make the seed grow. He can work every day scattering seed, but "the earth produces by itself." It works while he is sleeping. He has to sow faithfully and trust the seed and the soil to work without him. When it does grow, his job is to harvest.

I can't make anyone come to salvation. I can't reach inside people's hearts and cause them to be born again by the Spirit of God. That is a supernatural work beyond me. Even when God works through me to heal the sick or give prophetic words, I can't control how those things impact someone's heart. I could tell numerous stories of people receiving verifiable healing or words of knowledge but rejecting the gospel.

I scatter the seed. I sow the Word of God into the soil, and I want to be as effective at that as I can be. But I cannot make anything grow. The Holy Spirit does that. Understanding this represented a huge breakthrough in evangelism, discipleship, and my own growth and sanctification.

How does the heart change? How does the truth move from the head to the heart and become real in someone's life?

God does it.

God touches our lives by His Holy Spirit. In the same way that I can't make someone else's faith grow and transform their life, I can't reach inside my own heart and change it the way I want. All I have is the seed. So I scatter it. I scatter it in other's lives. I scatter it in my own.

I saturate my life with the gospel. I saturate my life with the Scripture. I saturate my life with the presence of God. I saturate my life with prayer. I scatter the seed on my own heart, and I trust the Lord to make it grow.

God made promises about our hearts in the New Covenant. He promised to perform His work within us:

> **Ezekiel 11:19-20 –** And I will give them one heart, and a new spirit I will put within them. I will remove the heart of stone from their flesh and give them a heart of flesh, that they may walk in My statutes and keep My rules and obey them. And they shall be My people, and I will be their God.

At salvation we received a new heart. Our old heart of stone was removed, and we received new desires to obey God. God did this as a one-time event, yet we walk in the freedom to choose. We have been made the stewards of this new heart. Like our new identity in Christ, we have a responsibility to live out of the desires of the Spirit within us, rather than the old desires of the flesh. This is the conflict within us.

> **Ezekiel 36:25-29 –** I will sprinkle clean water on you, and you shall be clean from all your uncleannesses, and from all your idols I will cleanse you. And I will give you a new heart, and a new spirit I will put within you. And I will remove the heart of stone from your flesh and give you a heart of flesh. And I will put My Spirit within you, and cause you to walk in My statutes and be careful to obey My rules. You shall dwell in the land that I gave to your fathers, and you shall be My people, and I will be your God. And I will deliver you from all your uncleannesses.

God promises to do His part in our hearts and lives. This is the growth and the transformation that we cannot control. God is the One who cleanses. God is the One who forgives. God is the One who provides a new heart with new desires. He gives the Spirit, and He initiates a new relationship where we belong to Him and He belongs to us as our God. In the midst of this new heart and new relationship with Him, we experience the deliverance from all our uncleanness.

> **Jeremiah 31:31-34 –** For this is the covenant that I will make with the house of Israel after those days, declares the Lord: I will put My law within them, and I will write it on their hearts. And I will be their God, and they shall be My people. And no longer shall each one teach his

195

neighbor and each his brother, saying, 'Know
the Lord,' for they shall all know Me, from the
least of them to the greatest, declares the Lord.
For I will forgive their iniquity, and I will
remember their sin no more."

This New Covenant is one of knowing God and relating to Him in personal experience. This is a covenant of fellowship and relationship. It is a covenant of prophetic community, where all involved know and experience God. We know His desires because He writes them on our hearts. We offer our hearts to Him; we surrender our desires to Him, and He writes new ones on the inside of us. This is an amazing promise, and it is work for which God takes responsibility. We simply need to know and relate to Him, walking in this New Covenant of faith.

God promises to do these things and takes responsibility for our hearts, yet the Bible does not teach that we have no part to play. James writes, "Purify your hearts, you double-minded" (James 4:8b).

God provides a new heart, but we must receive it. We must cast away our old works and repent of sins. We cannot hold onto our old hearts and old desires. We must let them go. This is the walk of repentance and faith. God works with us to make our hearts new. We surrender and submit to the process of change. We give ourselves to the Word. We submit to God. We offer our hearts to Him, and He gives new desires. We receive those desires and walk them out. We don't have the power to change our hearts without God. But with God we can repent and receive the new heart and new desires that He has for us.

They are already provided in the Spirit. They are in the seed that we have been given. Will we sow and care for that seed?

We know that the farmer does not grow the plants. The seed and the soil grow by the laws of nature. If the farmer's field is empty, it is usually because he did not plant. When we talk about farming, we sometimes talk about nature's work, and we sometimes talk about the farmer's work. We sometimes speak as if the farmer grows things himself. We sometimes speak as if it is out of his control. We understand that it is a synergy and a collaboration of our work and nature's work. In the same way, God has done the work and is working now, partnering with us to transform our hearts.

The process of sanctification and transformation is a relationship. It is a walk and talk with Jesus as He works within our hearts. He pushes the gospel into the dark places. He shines His light within. He expands His rule and His reign within us. That is His work. Our work is to walk and talk with Him—to relate to Him. It is to receive His Word and allow it to fill our lives. We listen. We pray. We read. We hear. And as we do, Christ works within.

We have many responsibilities and practical actions that we can take in our walk with God. This book touches on several of them. Faith and transformation involve our will, our choice, and our obedience. The heart and the will to do them is God's miracle-work within us.

We can't touch and change our own hearts, but we can touch the One who does. We can walk close to Jesus and trust His Word and His presence to produce growth and transformation in our lives.

You can't really know your identity in Christ from a

book. You can't really receive repentance by reading words or going through motions or steps. These are seeds. Hopefully they are potent seeds of truth and obedience that will have their way in your life. We must trust the process of scattering, watering, and growth as we wait for the harvest of holiness and maturity in our lives.

This doesn't always look the same. For some it comes suddenly in a dream or a vision, in a breakthrough moment, or at an altar call. For some it happens gradually in everyday study of Scripture or in a quiet moment of prayer. This is the work the Lord does in His way that is perfect for us. Our responsibility is to receive His work and position ourselves to receive the seeds well.

We partner with Christ to sow into our own lives. We go to Him. We say, "Speak to my heart, Lord." We open the Scripture. We listen with our spiritual ears and look with our spiritual eyes. We groan within with words that can't be uttered, longing to be changed into the more perfect and more glorious image of Christ in our daily lives. We see and believe in what Christ has done, and we long to live it out.

As we wait and as we grow, we walk with Jesus. We experience Him. We listen to Him. We receive His word day after day. We fill our lives with His truth, and somehow, often in moments we miss, that truth comes alive in our hearts, and faith is born. We suddenly know who we are beyond words on a page or recitations in our heads. We know it in our hearts.

ACTION STEP

Ask God:

What seed are You sowing in my heart?

Is there anything in my life that is choking out Your words like weeds or thorns?

If so, what are the names of those thorns?

How are You dealing with these issues in my life?

What is my specific, right-now part to play in removing these things from my life?

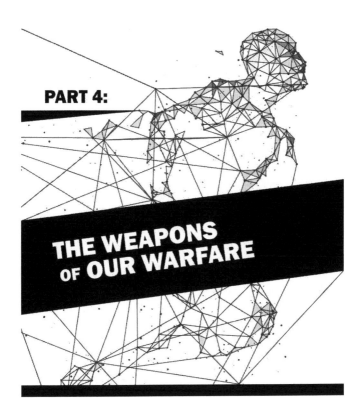

PART 4:

THE WEAPONS OF OUR WARFARE

We are in a fight for the truth. God's voice isn't the only voice speaking. We don't fight unarmed. God's voice equips us. We participate in the revelation of His truth in our lives. His voice overlaps with ours. Ours with His. We join Him in expressing His truth and beauty to the cosmos.

As we align our hearts and voices with His, we overcome our past, our circumstances, and our enemy.

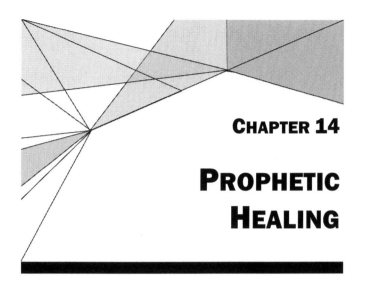

CHAPTER 14

PROPHETIC HEALING

I lay in bed exhausted. My travel schedule had kept me awake for over thirty hours. As I closed my eyes, I went into a vision. Similar to the night before I was born again, God took me through a stream of memories that came into focus one by one. Each memory involved how I perceived relationships with women. As I recognized the lies sown deep into the tapestry of my memory, each scene was peeled away.

God took me to the time in high school when I hit a girl in the face. It was peeled away. God took me to memories of the pornography addiction and all the times I had viewed abuse with pleasure. It was peeled away. He took me to the moment when I rejected a relationship with a girl and peeled away the guilt. He took me to a moment when I felt rejected. He peeled it away. God said, "Now you're free." And I knew it was true.

I instantly and deeply knew it was true. It went straight into my heart. It remains one of the most pivotal events of my life. I didn't ask for it at the time. I wasn't going through counseling or trying to forgive anyone. I was simply praying a lot, and the Lord knew it was time. He touched my heart when it was needed. He sent His word, and He healed me.

FORGETTING THE PAST

The Bible is clear that the old has passed away and that the new has come (2 Corinthians 5:17). All that went before has been nailed to the cross—that includes our family heritage, our past, our wounds, our habits, and our faults. We are free to begin again.

The Bible is also clear that we are in a process of growth. We are growing into all that Christ has done and aligning ourselves with His finished work.

> **1 Peter 2:2 –** Like newborn infants, long for the pure spiritual milk, that by it you may grow up into salvation. (ESV)

We are growing up into salvation. We are increasing and going from glory to glory until we attain the perfection Christ has accomplished in the spiritual realm.

> **Philippians 3:12-14 –** Not that I have already attained, or am already perfected; but I press on, that I may lay hold of that for which Christ Jesus has also laid hold of me. Brethren, I do not count myself to have apprehended; but one thing I do, forgetting those things which are behind and reaching forward to those things which are ahead, I press toward the goal for the

prize of the upward call of God in Christ Jesus.

The Apostle Paul had a horrifying past to overcome. He had persecuted the church and consented to martyring Stephen. He had broken up families and dragged off husbands and family members to prison. He had violently and aggressively attacked the Church of the Lord Jesus Christ. Yet years later he stood before that same church in Jerusalem and preached and taught as an apostle. It must have taken an incredible revelation of our death and resurrection in Christ to enable him to forget the past and move on to the future.

Paul did not claim present perfection. Instead he claimed a singleness of mind and motivation to turn from what went before and move on into the image of Christ. He was pressing on.

God's voice redirects us from the past to the future, moving us from what died on the cross to what is alive in God. Sometimes the voice of our past seems to speak louder than the voice of Jesus. It has been so written on our hearts and lives that it takes an encounter with the voice of God to set us free.

Jesus promised that the Holy Spirit is upon Him "to heal the brokenhearted" (Luke 4:18). Jesus sees the pain and the wounds of the heart. He sees how the past is still impacting our future. He heals. He restores health. His Spirit renews our minds so that we can forget what has gone before. Who we are and how we behave is cut off from what has been done to us. Jesus continues this ministry until He wipes every tear from every eye and "death shall be no more, neither shall there be mourning, nor crying, nor pain anymore, for the former things have passed away" (Revelations 21:4).

Every sin issue can be destroyed through simple repentance and faith in the truth. Though the answer is always the same—the cross and resurrection of Jesus Christ—there are many ways to evangelize the human heart. Freedom and repentance can be found through God's prophetic healing of past wounds, bitterness, guilt, and shame.

Sin is always our responsibility. Parents and circumstances are not responsible for our choice to sin. It is our own sinful responses that create wounds, and it is our own unbelief and resistance to the work of Christ that keeps them after we have been born again. Many have horrendously tragic and traumatic pasts but live free and whole in Christ today. They have never had a distinct experience where God's voice set them free from their past. They either responded righteously through their circumstance, preventing wounds from forming, or they simply believed the full truth when they received Christ.

Similarly, those with relatively healthy pasts often struggle with wounds, not because they experienced a uniquely difficult past but because their unrighteous responses to their circumstances formed wounds. This does not mean that the trauma is the victim's fault. It does mean that in order to be whole we must respond and continue to respond to our past with Christ's grace. Many things that happen to us are not our fault. They are unjust and evil. Jesus has made a way for us to be free and whole from every trauma. We are responsible to take the path to freedom.

As we fill our hearts with God's Word, He speaks to past wounds. He binds them up and heals them. Joseph named his son Mannaseh, which means "causing to forget." "'For,' he said, 'God has made me forget all my hardship and all my father's house'" (Genesis 41:51). God's action healed Joseph's heart from the hardship of his past, his family life, and the trauma of his youth.

We don't forget what we have been through. Our past stands as a testimony of what God has done. We do, however, "forget" the pain and trauma of the past. We no longer experience that pain and trauma in the present. Our thoughts and emotions align with the truth.

The Psalmist wrote, "For my father and my mother have forsaken me, but the Lord will take me in" (Psalm 27:10). Regardless of who you have been or what you have done, God the Father will take you in. We all suffered from growing up and being formed in this fallen world. We have a chance to begin again in the family of God—a family that will never cast us out.

TRUTH TO LIES

I once prophesied over a friend that she was an archer, that even as the enemy had fiery darts, that she also had a quiver full of flaming arrows to shoot and intercept the lies of the enemy through prophecy.

That is often how the Spirit works. The enemy sees the past as a goldmine for convincing lies. He can use a number of places in our history to craft a lie that keeps us bound in who we once were and what we experienced rather than in the revelation of who we now are in Christ. The Spirit works to intercept those lies by revealing their roots, exposing them, and speaking the truth. Many times the Spirit will simply identify and speak healing to the issue. At other times He requires our partnership to reject a lie we have believed. He will prompt us to forgive others and renounce the lies and strongholds that have formed in our hearts.

The cross cut us off from the wounds of our past two thousand years ago. Today we are defined by the gospel and our relationship with Christ. We have the DNA of the Father, and we are at home with Him. This new home-life teaches us to live as children of God. Our earthly home-lives may have taught us many lies, but our relationship with God redefines everything.

We still have the memories and experiences of who we were before the cross. We still have a mind influenced by our old life. This why we must renew our mind in the Word of God and the voice of the Spirit. God reminds us that we are not who we were. We are neither nature nor nurture. We are spirit beings with a new life in Christ. Day by day the Spirit prompts us to reject lies we learned through experience and receive the truth found in Him.

> **Isaiah 53:4-6 –** Yet it was our grief He bore, our sorrows that weighed Him down. And we thought His troubles were a punishment from God, for His own sins! But He was wounded and bruised for our sins. He was chastised that we might have peace; He was lashed – and we were healed! We are the ones who strayed like sheep! We, who left God's paths to follow our own. Yet God laid on Him, the guilt and sins of every one of us! (TLB)

Christ bore our grief and sorrow. He was beaten for our peace at the cross. He took our shame upon Himself. As new creations in Christ, the past has no grip on us. We truly are new, but occasionally we fail to surrender some part of our hearts or experience to the cross. The Holy Spirit speaks to that dark place of our heart where we refuse to be new, and He gives us the tools to experience the forgiveness, deliverance, and healing of our whole man.

RENEWAL

When the Holy Spirit reveals lies, He does so to inspire us to repent. We have to turn away from allowing wounds to define us or to dictate our behavior. God has opened the prison door. We must walk out. God has raised us from the dead; we must remove the grave clothes. We must renew our minds to the truth and renounce the lies life has taught us. We must forgive and release others so we can be freed ourselves.

When God identifies wounds from our past, He is identifying lies that we have believed. Such a lie may be that we are unloved or shameful. It may be that we are unworthy or dirty. It may be that we are rejected. It may be, as in my case, that we are evil and abusive. God intercepts these lies with His truth. We must accept what He says and renounce the lie that we have believed. This can be as simple as a verbal confession.

> Lord, because of what has happened in my past I have believed a lie that _____. I renounce this lie in Jesus' name. I confess the truth that _____ in the name of Jesus.

Often, dealing with the past requires forgiveness.

Bitterness and refusing to forgive bind us to the past. They hold on to what has been done to us as relevant to our current life. They say that God's justice on the cross was not enough. They say that God's forgiveness is not enough. They say that the blood of Jesus is not enough.

Refusing to forgive also says that we deserve to be forgiven and others don't. It blasphemes the cross and the blood of Christ. Jesus said multiple times that refusing to forgive leads to Hell. "But if you do not forgive men their trespasses, neither will your Father forgive your trespasses" (Matthew 6:15; See Mark 11:26). Jesus finished a famous parable about forgiveness with this warning:

> **Matthew 18:34-35 –** And his master was angry, and delivered him to the torturers until he should pay all that was due to him.
> "So My heavenly Father also will do to you if each of you, from his heart, does not forgive his brother his trespasses."

Forgiveness is the difference between health and torture. Refusing to forgive wrecks souls. Forgiveness is the most consistent way I have seen instant freedom and deliverance from sin and oppression. Often physical healing accompanies forgiveness. Forgiving others acknowledges the truth of the Gospel. We have received an incomparable and incomprehensible wealth of grace and forgiveness. To withhold forgiveness is injustice.

> **Isaiah 43:25 –** The Lord says, "I am He who blots out your transgressions for My own sake, and I will not remember your sins." (ESV)

Hebrews 8:12 – "For I will be merciful toward their iniquities, and I will remember their sins no more."

With the cleansing blood of Jesus comes forgiveness for us and for others. His blood cleanses us from all unrighteousness (1 John 1:9). This means both unrighteousness that we have done and unrighteousness done to us—all unrighteousness. God has cleansing and healing for every heart and for every wound. Every issue of the past has been nailed to the cross. Christ binds up our wounds and pours the oil of His Spirit and the wine of His blood upon them. You are free to forgive and forget what has gone before and press on to the beauty of what lies ahead.

ACTION STEP

Ask God:

Are there any lies I've believed from my past?

Renounce them:

Lord, because of what has happened in my past, I have believed that _____. I renounce this lie in Jesus's name. I confess the truth that _____ in the name of Jesus.

Take some time to quietly ask the Lord if there is anyone you need to forgive. Pray through the following "Forgiveness and Freedom Prayer" for that person. (If the Lord did not speak to you about anyone, pick someone who you have had to forgive in the past, and practice the "Forgiveness and Freedom Prayer" for them.)

Forgiveness and Freedom Prayer[1]

Lord, there are people who have hurt me. Some of them have done it on purpose. Right now, I choose to forgive them.

(*Think of the people you are forgiving by name. Speak their names*)

Lord, all those people I just forgave, I release them. I want them to live a happy life.

They don't owe me anything.

I don't want them punished.

I don't want them dead.

I want You, Lord, to treat them as if they had never harmed me.

Give me the grace to have no hard feelings toward them. I receive Your peace.

In Jesus' name, Amen.

---

[1] The concept for this prayer came from a prayer I heard in a sermon on forgiveness. It has been adapted as I've used it over the years.

CHAPTER 15

PROPHETIC WARFARE

"**Y**ou can't cast me out!" The demon said in the man's voice.

I laughed.

Casting out demons is not funny to me. Seeing anyone in bondage to the devil provokes both anger and compassion, but when I heard the demon say that we couldn't cast him out, it struck me as funny. Demons lie, and the devil lies. I knew that the demon had to submit to Christ's authority and bow to the name of Jesus. Anything else seemed ludicrous. The demon left the man a moment later.

> **John 8:44** – You are of your father the devil, and the desires of your father you want to do. He was a murderer from the beginning, and does not stand in the truth, because there is no truth in him. When he speaks a lie, he speaks from his own resources, for he is a liar and the father of it.

Satan lies. The devil and demons are deceivers. Their language is lies. They do not have useful information and are not worth talking to.

When I was a teenager, I spent several years interacting with the devil on a regular basis. I had recurring dreams where demons came in the middle of the night and brought me to Satan where we interacted. These dreams occurred every night for months, and I continued having them frequently until I gave my life to Christ.

I have no interest in Satan. He has no part of me, and I want nothing to do with him. He is not mysterious. If I do interact with demons, my goal is to cast them out as quickly as possible and to allow them to speak and act as little as possible. Any fascination with the devil comes from Satan's own propaganda about himself.

Satan tries to defeat us because he is defeated. He lies because he is deceived. He confuses because he is confused. He binds others because he is bound. He inspires fear because he is afraid. He depresses because he is depressed.

Our culture makes heroes out of the depressed and suicidal. Satan has weaved a lie into popular culture that those who kill themselves have deeper passions than the rest of us. People become proud of their struggles with the demonic.

Satan attempts to scare and seduce those who see and discern in the spirit realm by making himself visible and using intimidation and temptation to trap the prophetically gifted into focusing on him. Many of the prophetic people who regularly teach on spiritual warfare or deliverance tend to have an unhealthy obsession with the devil. But he is tiny compared to Jesus and often not worth mentioning.

As many teachers point out, "Discerning of spirits is not the discerning of devils." The Holy Spirit gives gifts so that we can interact with Him, the Body of Christ, and the lost, and also to destroy the works of the devil. If you are discerning the work of the devil without discerning and applying the Solution, you are drawing attention to the enemy, and he loves attention.

By giving the devil attention and attributing power to him, we disable ourselves from confronting him as we should. We begin to focus on the work of the enemy rather than on the work of the Spirit. We focus on Satan's lies instead of truth.

When we are engaged in personal spiritual warfare, we must hold on to the revelation of Christ's victory and treat the enemy as a defeated foe regardless of our circumstances. When all else fails, ignoring the enemy can be an effective strategy:

> **Philippians 1:28 –** ...without being frightened in any way by those who oppose you. This is a sign to them that they will be destroyed, but that you will be saved—and that by God.

There are a number of instances where Satan and demonic forces are overcome by recognizing, "Oh, it's just Satan," and continuing on with our day and our walk with God. We are not only not to be frightened, but we are not to be frightened "in any way."

Years after I was saved, demons would still attempt to visit me at night. They couldn't do anything like what they did before I was saved, but they would come into the room and attempt to disturb me. Eventually, someone brought this verse to my attention, and I learned to ignore the demons I saw, roll over, and go back to sleep. I often didn't even acknowledge their presence. I decided not to be frightened in any way. If I had a nightmare, I would yawn and roll over. I didn't care. These events lost all their power. Demons stopped showing up.

This principle applies to personal struggles, deliverance ministry, and prophetic revelation. Regardless of what we are dealing with, we should not be alarmed, disturbed, or dismayed by the presence and work of the enemy. We should take it seriously, and we should not be lax or foolish; but if we are intimidated by the devil, then we approach the battlefield as losers.

Christ has already won. He is leading us in triumph even now. The battle is over. This is the celebration. That is the revelation from which we live and speak.

If we are intimidated by the devil, he will attempt to flood our spiritual eyes and ears in hopes of drowning out the truth with impressive revelations of his activity that only distract us from being fruitful. We are messengers of Christ, not messengers of the devil. We speak and prophesy what God is doing. The prophetic identifies the devil's work in order to destroy it. The devil's power is in deception. When he is revealed accurately through the voice of God, he loses his power and ability to deceive. Satan is always revealed as weak.

When we perceive the demonic, we often have strong negative feelings. Often when dealing with demons, an alarm goes off in my spirit. Shivers go down my spine. The hair on the back of my neck stands on end. These are powerful feelings, but that does not mean demons are powerful.

I once heard someone use this analogy: If you stepped into a locker room and the air was so filled with sweat and body odor that it was nearly overpowering, you might assume that powerful, professional athletes dressed there. You would be embarrassed if moments later, scrawny, middle-school boys entered after their gym class. Just because something has a powerful smell doesn't mean that it is powerful.

Intimidation is one of Satan's few weapons. It is a cheap trick. Don't believe it, and don't extol the devil's power, strength, or craftiness. The devil was stripped of his power by Jesus Christ, is already a defeated foe, and lives in confusion. He is a liar. God has given us authority over all of his ability (Luke 10:19). Jesus stripped him of the keys of hell, death, and the grave.

WELCOME TO THE WAR

> **Ephesians 6:12** – For we do not wrestle against flesh and blood, but against principalities, against powers, against the rulers of the darkness of this age, against spiritual hosts of wickedness in the heavenly places.

The Bible is clear that the devil and demons are both real and "personal." They are not mere forces without an identity; they are individual beings. The devil exists to steal, kill, and destroy (John 10:10). While we cannot give the devil undue attention, we must be balanced and acknowledge that every single believer's pursuit of holiness will involve warfare with the enemy.

219

Satan harasses us with temptation. He whispers, "Do it. It will be fun. Do it. It will bring relief. Do it. God will forgive you later. Do it. No one will know. Do it. You deserve it. Do it." He speaks over and over, trying to wear us down. If we give in, he immediately changes his game to condemnation. He whispers, "You did it. You are condemned. You did it. God hates you. You did it. You are going to hell. You did it. You are an addict. You did it. It doesn't matter if you do it again." He creates cycles of sin, guilt, and condemnation. He uses these tactics over and over, yet so often we fail to recognize his lying voice in the midst of desire and shame.

It doesn't matter what visions you have. It doesn't matter how well you know your identity in Christ. It doesn't matter how much Scripture you have memorized or how free you are from the past. You will have to resist the devil. You will have to resist temptation. You will have to renounce his lies and say "no" to sin.

When I was a new believer, I read a number of biographies that led me to believe that I could have some sort of spiritual experience that would free me from temptation. This is not true. Temptation will always come. You will always have to resist the devil. And God has given you a way of escape. He has given you the power to resist. You can be free.

> **1 Corinthians 10:13 –** No temptation has overtaken you except such as is common to man; but God is faithful, who will not allow you to be tempted beyond what you are able, but with the temptation will also make the way of escape, that you may be able to bear it.

You are not unique in your temptations. It doesn't

matter how strange or perverted you may feel or your temptation may seem. It is "common to man." This means that others experience it too. Others have been tempted and resisted. Others have been through the same moment you have, and they have overcome.

Jesus was tempted in every way and still was without sin (Hebrews 4:15). As weak and bound as you may feel, you have the power to resist and walk in victory. God has given you a specific way of escape. You have a way out. God has provided a plan for you to leave temptation. No temptation lasts forever, and when it is over, you will have won. Take God's escape route. Endure the temptation. Outlast the devil.

Temptation is suffering. Temptation hurts. The pull and call of our desires put us into conflict that tears at us. We have not resisted to the point of shedding of blood. Jesus has (Hebrews 9:22). Jesus endured the full pain and suffering of temptation because He never gave in. When we reach our limit, we fall. Jesus has no limits and never sinned. He took the full brunt of unfulfilled desire and still turned His back on sin. That same Jesus lives in and through you. He will not resist sin for you. He gives you His power to resist sin. You have access to His strength.

As you resist the devil, you will grow in victory and in the power of the Spirit. The devil will flee from you, and temptation will become easier and easier to overcome. You will grow and gain momentum in the battle. But Satan will still return to try you again. "Now when the devil had ended every temptation, he departed from [Jesus] until an opportune time" (Luke 4:13, emphasis added). You will have to learn to take up the weapons of our warfare and stand firm.

TAKING EVERY THOUGHT CAPTIVE

> **James 1:12-15 –** Blessed is the man who
> endures temptation; for when he has been
> approved, he will receive the crown of life,
> which the Lord has promised to those who love
> Him. Let no one say when he is tempted, "I am
> tempted by God"; for God cannot be tempted
> by evil, nor does He Himself tempt anyone. But
> each one is tempted when he is drawn away by
> his own desires and enticed. Then, when desire
> has conceived, it gives birth to sin; and sin,
> when it is full-grown, brings forth death.

Because I did not want to consider the devil when I was young in the faith, I considered all sin, temptation, depression, and negative thoughts to purely come from within my own heart.

James writes that we are tempted when we are carried away by our own lust. Sin is our personal responsibility. However, Jesus Himself was tempted, and He had no lusts that stained Him with sin. He simply had a human body and difficult circumstances. Satan used those to tempt Him.

Temptation does not mean that we are sinful or sinning. I used to feel guilty and condemned every time a wrong thought went through my head, believing that it was coming from an impure heart. While it's true that the impurity of our hearts can produce evil thoughts and draw us into lust, those who are born again and genuine in their faith should have a general purity of heart.

Not every thought that comes into your mind is

your own. I am putting thoughts in your head right now as you read these words. If I start talking about pink elephants, you will immediately begin to think about pink elephants. The same is true when I talk about sex or money. The same is true when our spiritual adversaries come and speak to us about the desires of the flesh. When someone communicates to you, their expressed thoughts enter your mind. When the Holy Spirit speaks to you, His voice becomes processed in your mind and thoughts. The same is true for the enemy.

I don't believe that every time you have a wrong or tempting thought it is the devil himself whispering in your ear—he does not exist everywhere at once like God. I also do not believe that it is a literal demon, though it certainly could be. I believe there are a finite number of demons. Satan attempts to weave his lies into culture and lifestyle so that they come out and attack us simply because this fallen world is saturated with lies.

It could be that the thought originates with us and isn't demonic at all. An example I frequently use is the voice of our bodies. My body does not know right from wrong and never will. My body is not evil, but its desires have to be ruled because it has no moral direction. If I see a sandwich, my body wants to eat it regardless of who owns the sandwich. My body's desires are not affected by morality. My body would gladly steal a sandwich and eat it to satisfy my hunger. Lustful thoughts and other selfish desires often arise from our body's natural desires. These desires are not wrong, but they need to be ruled; and though the body doesn't learn moral desires, it can be trained to obey.

By discerning our thoughts and intentions, we wage

warfare in the Spirit, denying the work and desire of the devil and resisting him. Regardless of where thoughts come from—whether the world, the flesh, or the devil— we should take every thought captive to the obedience of Christ, meaning each thought should motivate us to obedience (2 Corinthians 10:5). Discernment becomes identifying with the mind of Christ. Is this a thought that Christ would embrace or reject? If Christ rejects it, then so do I. The thoughts that pass through my mind do not identify me any more than what someone says to me identifies me. I get to choose what I receive or reject. By knowing who I am in Christ and maintaining a pure heart, I reject lies and embrace truth. I recognize Jesus and the voice of the Holy Spirit and refuse to follow the voice of a stranger.

Jesus said, "And when he brings out his own sheep, he goes before them; and the sheep follow him, for they know his voice. Yet they will by no means follow a stranger, but will flee from him, for they do not know the voice of strangers" (John 10:4-5).

In this teaching, Jesus did not say that we would not hear a stranger's voice. He said we would not follow it. This means not all the voices we hear are from God. Not all the voices we hear are from ourselves; many are from the fallen realm—earthly or demonic. We don't beat ourselves up for hearing the call of a stranger. Instead we take warning and refuse to follow that call, reminding ourselves who we are.

Jesus answered the voice of the devil with the voice of God. He spoke the Word of God into each temptation, disarming it (see Luke 4:1-15). As we know the Word more and more, we are more specific and more effective in wielding the Sword of the Spirit. Regardless of how much of the Bible you know, if you know God, you can begin to disarm temptation with His truth. You can speak the truth to Satan's lies. The lies of the enemy have the same basic foundations. He casts doubt on what God says. You can respond by saying, "God, I trust You. I believe You. I may not understand everything, but I'm going to follow You in purity of faith."

Satan casts doubts on God's goodness. You can respond with worship: "God, I love You. You're awesome. You're holy. You are true. You are good. You are good to me. You love me. You fill my life with good things." Even only a small piece of revelation that you have about God can be a powerful weapon against the enemy. Allow his lies to push you further into your love-relationship with Jesus and your dedication to God's truth.

Jesus was led by the Spirit into the wilderness and into temptation. He went in filled with the Holy Spirit. He left the wilderness full of the Holy Spirit and the Spirit's power (Luke 4:14). Consecrating ourselves and resisting temptation prepares us for power. If we resist the devil, he will flee from us. If we live a life of resisting the devil, we gain a reputation, and he will flee people's lives when we come into their proximity. Our personal victory over Satan prepares us to set the captives free. We should be ready to receive an upgrade every time we enter temptation.

LIBERTY FOR THE CAPTIVES

In the same way that discerning between the voice of Jesus and the voice of a stranger enables us to live holy, so discerning the work of the devil in our lives and the lives of others can set people free from oppression and bondage. God often gives words of knowledge that people are experiencing depression, anxiety, or some other form of emotional oppression. While these things can temporarily be brought on by normal circumstances, ongoing conditions of bondage may be demonic oppression.

Jesus ministered a few solutions to many problems. He preached and taught, and this includes the numerous prophecies He gave. Jesus only spoke the words of God. Along with this ministry of the Word were two applications: He healed, and He cast out demons.

I fully believe that these simple solutions still answer every problem. Many times, you can minister freedom through simple teaching. At other times an exhortation of faith is required. Physical healing addresses issues in the body, and deliverance addresses the demonic.

We should use all wisdom and be practical in our pursuit of health and freedom. I had serious insomnia for years and wasn't free until I began to exercise regularly. Sometimes practical wisdom is what we need. Our world is filled with damaging input from what we choose for entertainment to what we choose for dessert. Allow God to reveal what is demonic and what comes from foolish choices.

Today we have so many diagnoses and so many labels and theories about the location and root of problems that we drown ourselves in the problem, rather than minister the solution. Things like depression and anxiety must bow to the name of Jesus. This can happen in a variety of ways. You can teach someone to refuse depression. They may be freed by exercise and sunshine. You can preach and impart strength into their spirit until the revelation of faith overwhelms the condition. If the depression is caused by a physical issue, you can minister healing to the process of the chemicals of the brain. Often you can cast a spirit of depression away.

Jesus named spirits according to what they did and cast them away. Today, you and I have that same authority. That authority can manifest in a simple command: "Depression, go in Jesus' name." This may not provide permanent relief as the person must learn to walk in their own authority over depression, but it can break the momentum of the condition and give time to recover ground and gain a healthy place above the oppression.

Satan tempted Jesus, prefacing each temptation with, "If you are the Son of God." He wanted to cast doubt on Christ's identity. Jesus answered him with God's word. He answered with what God had said about Him.

The written Word of God gives strength to each of us as we make it personal to our lives. The prophetic strengthens us as we receive the specific word of Christ for our lives. The voice of God drowns out the lies of the enemy, and what God says about us becomes larger than every lie and temptation. Truth sets us free and binds the enemy.

ACTION STEP

Are you aware of any specific lies that the devil has tried to tell you or harass you with?

Do you have any persistent thoughts that bother you or cause you shame?

Ask God:

What is the lie in this thought?

Spend time praising God, thanking Him, and rejoicing that the opposite of that lie is true.

> If lust is the issue, praise God that He is working to make you pure in Him.

> If condemnation is the issue, praise God out loud that you are accepted in Him and that He will never cast you out.

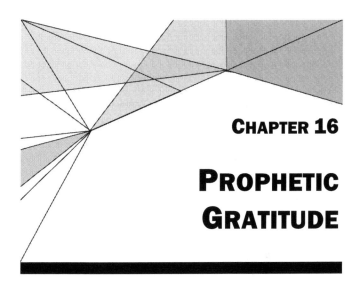

CHAPTER 16

PROPHETIC GRATITUDE

I had been praying and walking for two hours, and by the end I had completely descended into complaining. I was completely broke. I had no money. While I had no debt, I was going to have to start using my credit card. Someone had rolled under my car in the middle of the night with a pipe cutter and stolen my catalytic converter. My ministry was experiencing "donor fatigue," and financial support was not coming in. I had lived below the poverty line for most of my time in full-time ministry, and I was fed up.

What the heck, God. I've been full-time for six years, and now I'm going to have to get a job at McDonald's. I don't get it. I've given faithfully since I've been saved. I knocked on 300 doors this month to share Jesus with people. Muslims have made decisions for Christ this year. We've seen miracles. But I'm broke. So-and-so is on full-time support; they live here and they have more than enough. They never share the gospel. This isn't fair.

My thoughts can get pretty ugly. And this was after a long time of prayer.

God reminded me of Luke 17:7-10:

> And which of you, having a servant plowing or tending sheep, will say to him when he has come in from the field, 'Come at once and sit down to eat'? But will he not rather say to him, 'Prepare something for my supper, and gird yourself and serve me till I have eaten and drunk, and afterward you will eat and drink'? Does he thank that servant because he did the things that were commanded him? I think not. So likewise you, when you have done all those things which you are commanded, say, 'We are unprofitable servants. We have done what was our duty to do.'

I apologized to the Lord. I have only done what God had called me to do. I have only done what I should. I'm not in it for the money, and I can't earn my pay. God provides.

I started to thank God for His mercy in my life. I thanked Him for forgiveness. I thanked Him for grace. I thanked Him for calling me. I thanked Him for all the miracles that He had done for me. I thanked God for His provision. I thanked God that I hadn't missed a meal.

As I lay in bed that night, I stared at a cross necklace hanging on my wall. I had been such a sissy. There were believers in China hiding from the government at that moment. There were believers being beaten and abused. There were Christians who were hungry, and didn't know where their next meal was coming from. They still witnessed. They still worshipped. They still gave thanks to God. I was soft. I was weak. I could barely go through a small trial without whining. I thanked God for His incredible kindness and patience toward me.

The next week, I received two financial miracles.

The Bible teaches that ingratitude is a source of sin and judgment in our lives. The Israelites were delivered from Egypt, but they complained because they were thirsty and hungry. God supernaturally provided food and water, but they complained because it tasted boring. They died in the wilderness.

Paul wrote that ingratitude and failing to give God glory became the downfall of the human race:

> **Romans 1:8-25 –** For the wrath of God is revealed from heaven against all ungodliness and unrighteousness of men, who suppress the truth in unrighteousness, because what may be known of God is manifest in them, for God has shown it to them. For since the creation of the world His invisible attributes are clearly seen, being understood by the things that are made, even His eternal power and Godhead, so that they are without excuse, because, although they knew God, they did not glorify Him as God, nor were thankful, but became futile in their thoughts, and their foolish hearts were darkened. Professing to be wise, they became fools, and changed the glory of the incorruptible God into an image made like corruptible man— and birds and four-footed animals and creeping things.
>
> Therefore God also gave them up to uncleanness, in the lusts of their hearts, to dishonor their bodies among themselves, who

> exchanged the truth of God for the lie, and
> worshiped and served the creature rather than
> the Creator, who is blessed forever. Amen.

Romans states that God's wrath and judgment comes against the unrighteous because God's glory has been revealed, yet they have refused to acknowledge it. They knew God, but they refused to worship Him. The Bible illuminates their rebellion and attitude, but then points specifically to their actions: They did not glorify Him as God, nor were they thankful.

Paul was addressing humanity as a whole here and pointed to ingratitude as a source of sin and judgment. Ingratitude is the outworking of unbelief and evidence of a refusal to acknowledge God and spiritual reality. Ingratitude denies and suppresses the truth about God's goodness. Gratitude declares the truth.

Humanity's ingratitude led to worshipping idols. We were made to be worshippers. We cannot hold back our worship. We will pour it out on something. It may be weak or twisted, but we will worship idols (even ourselves) if we do not worship God. Our hearts will stray. Gratitude sets our hearts on God.

> **Romans 1:26-27 —** For this reason God gave
> them up to vile passions. For even their women
> exchanged the natural use for what is against
> nature. Likewise also the men, leaving the
> natural use of the woman, burned in their lust
> for one another, men with men committing
> what is shameful, and receiving in themselves
> the penalty of their error which was due.

Humanity's lack of worship caused Him to lift His hand of grace from them, and they cast off restraint. The Bible refers to sexual perversion as part of their idolatry and part of the consequences and penalty of refusing the truth about God. The cycle and spiral of sin begins with a lack of worship and thanksgiving to God and ends in a twisted perversion of what we were created to be. Our actions no longer demonstrate the goodness of God and His design, but refuse His words and twist His testimony to the universe.

> **Romans 1:28-31 –** And even as they did not like to retain God in their knowledge, God gave them over to a debased mind, to do those things which are not fitting; being filled with all unrighteousness, sexual immorality, wickedness, covetousness, maliciousness; full of envy, murder, strife, deceit, evil-mindedness; they are whisperers, backbiters, haters of God, violent, proud, boasters, inventors of evil things, disobedient to parents, undiscerning, untrustworthy, unloving, unforgiving, unmerciful; who, knowing the righteous judgment of God, that those who practice such things are deserving of death, not only do the same but also approve of those who practice them.

Thanksgiving renews and refreshes our minds in God's love and grace. Ingratitude gives our minds over to sin, which leads to sinful actions and bondage. If we are experiencing these sins in our lives, we can trace them back to idolatry and a lack of worship and thankfulness.

These sins result from not acknowledging God's power and goodness. Acknowledging God's power and goodness through worship and gratitude takes us back to the place of seeing God and recognizing the truth.

THANKSGIVING PROPHESIES

After the people of Israel escaped the Egyptians by walking through the Red Sea the Bible says, "When the people of Israel saw the mighty power that the Lord had unleashed against the Egyptians, they were filled with awe before Him. They put their faith in the Lord and in His servant Moses." The people of Israel had an appropriate response to the miracle. They believed God. They believed in His goodness and His power.

In the next verse they sing a song of thanks:

> **Exodus 15:1 –** Then Moses and the people of Israel sang this song to the Lord: I will sing to the Lord, for He has triumphed gloriously; He has hurled both horse and rider into the sea.

The song continued, describing what God has done, what God does, and what God will do. The praise and thanksgiving spanned from the past to the future. It revealed then who God is now, and it transcends time.

In Revelation, the victors in the last days sing this song of Moses and combine it with the song of the Lamb (Revelation 15:2-3). Moses's thanksgiving became a prophetic word that spans throughout time and continues into eternity because his praise accurately spoke of who God is. It speaks of His power. It speaks of His goodness. It speaks of His plan. It speaks of God's past goodness,

His present action, and His future promise. Our thanks can do the same.

In 1 Samuel, God answered Hannah's prayer for a son; she responded by praising God. She had made a vow to God that if He gave her a son, she would give him back to God. In 1 Samuel 2, the baby had just been given away. Samuel was no longer hers. Hannah rejoiced in God's promise, and her prayer of thanksgiving and praise can be found in that same chapter. Like Moses's song, Hannah's prayer recounts God's past, present, and future goodness. Her praise acknowledged God's power and goodness and prophesied His continued power and goodness in the lives of His people. Her prayer now stands as Scripture and a prophetic word for all.

Praise announces God's victory and deliverance. Thanksgiving begins with what God has done and, by faith and the Spirit of God, moves into what God will do. Praise predicts good things. Praise and thanksgiving send a message of strength and power into the future. Praise sets the captives free because it partners with God's power.

Mary, the mother of Jesus, gave praise to God when greeted by Elizabeth:

> **Luke 1:46-48** – And Mary said:
> "My soul magnifies the Lord,
> > And my spirit has rejoiced in God my
> > Savior.
> For He has regarded the lowly state of His
> > maidservant;
> For behold, henceforth all generations will
> > call me blessed.

Mary allowed her soul and her spirit to respond to

God's promise and prophetic word. Faith prompted her to shout out praise and thanks to God. In her praise, she announced God's prophetic plan and thanked Him for her part in it. She repeated God's promise: "…all generations will call me blessed." Praise and thanksgiving acknowledge and receive God's promises for us, including freedom and deliverance from sin. Thanksgiving and praise cut off the descent of our desires and realign our hearts with God.

In the same chapter of Luke, John the Baptist's father Zechariah prophesied; but his prophecy began with praise:

Now his father Zacharias was filled with the Holy Spirit, and prophesied, saying:

> **Luke 1:67-79 –** "Blessed is the Lord God of Israel,
> For He has visited and redeemed His people,
> And has raised up a horn of salvation for us
> In the house of His servant David,
> As He spoke by the mouth of His holy prophets,
> Who have been since the world began,
> That we should be saved from our enemies
> And from the hand of all who hate us,
> To perform the mercy promised to our fathers
> And to remember His holy covenant,
> The oath which He swore to our father
>   Abraham:
> To grant us that we,
> Being delivered from the hand of our enemies,
> Might serve Him without fear,
> In holiness and righteousness before Him all the
>   days of our life.
> "And you, child, will be called the prophet of the

Highest;

For you will go before the face of the Lord to
prepare His ways,

To give knowledge of salvation to His people

By the remission of their sins,

Through the tender mercy of our God,

With which the Dayspring from on high has
visited us;

To give light to those who sit in darkness and
the shadow of death,

To guide our feet into the way of peace."

Zechariah began by praising God for what He had done. He praised God that "…we, being delivered from the hand of our enemies, might serve Him without fear in holiness and righteousness before Him all the days of our life." This is something worth praising God for! We have been delivered from our enemies. Sin and death have been defeated. We are free to serve God without fear. We are free to serve Him in holiness and righteousness all the days of our life and forever and ever. Zechariah then began to predict John the Baptist's ministry. John preached repentance. Zechariah's word confirmed that John's ministry gave knowledge of salvation to God's people. John the Baptist's message was one of the remission of sins. Praise God!

The New Testament confirms this prophecy and praise, and we live in the fulfillment of these promises. God's character has been perfectly revealed in Jesus Christ, and we live in the love of the Father. We have even greater reason to acknowledge God's goodness and power. We have even greater opportunity for thanksgiving. Paul commanded us to be vigilant in giving thanks and praise to

God.

> **Colossians 4:2** – Continue earnestly in prayer, being vigilant in it with thanksgiving.

Thanksgiving is important. Praise is important. Giving God glory is important. These establish our hearts. They bring us into God's promise and blessing. They combat sin in our lives. They are a declaration of faith and freedom. Praise and thanksgiving are not to be taken lightly. We commend prayer and Bible reading as daily spiritual disciplines, and they are; but Paul commended vigilance in thanksgiving and partnered it with prayer.

We must give thanks. Free people give thanks. Holy people give thanks. Worshippers give thanks. We are those people, and we become those people by partnering with God's promise and prophetic word with praise.

Paul told the Corinthians in 2 Corinthians 4:14-16 that the purpose of the gospel and grace is that it "may cause thanksgiving to abound to the glory of God" (2 Corinthians 4:15). The result of grace in our lives should be thanks and praise. In Ephesians, "singing and making melody in your heart to the Lord" is the result of being filled with the Spirit.

Praise is the fruit of the Spirit-filled life, and we can make a choice to give thanks and praise God today. Paul ordered the Colossians to "always be thankful" (Colossians 3:15, NLT) and to "Sing psalms and hymns and spiritual songs to God with thankful hearts" (Colossians 3:16, NLT). These are the weapons of our warfare. Thanksgiving is part of our victory and part of our fight. Praise overcame armies in 2 Chronicles 20. Praise overcomes idolatry and sin in our lives.

I have heard numerous testimonies of men and women being set free from sin, anger, depression, and bondages through the power of praise, worship, and thanksgiving. We do these things for God. When we do, we position ourselves back into His design for our lives and our humanity. We were meant to testify to Jesus and to God's love and goodness forever. This speaks of what God has done, but it overflows into the prophetic testimony of the present and future. We speak praise, and God speaks future victory and life.

ACTION STEP

Think about what God has done. Lift your hands and praise Him, naming each thing you can think of.

Think about what God is doing in your life and heart right now. Lift your hands and praise Him, naming each thing.

Think about who God is and the promises He has made. Think about what God will do. Lift your hands and praise Him. Let yourself get carried away.

Reflect on the praise you just gave. Was it prophetic? Did it speak to the future?

CHAPTER 17

LOVE REVEALED

My good friends Andrew and Abby had just had their first child, and I went to the hospital with some other friends to see them and to see the baby for the first time. Both Andrew and Abby were exhausted and happy.

When Abby asked if I wanted to hold their newborn son, Levi, I took him from her gingerly and looked down at the baby in my arms. His eyes were squeezed shut. His mouth was in a hard line. An unexplainable joy washed over me. Levi felt like one of the greatest miracles I had ever seen.

This was a human being we had never met before—one who couldn't speak or introduce himself. And we loved him.

He was loved just because he was. He had done nothing to make us love him. There was no reason for this love. This person had arrived, and we immediately loved him. I thought this must be what God feels. He loves us just because we are.

Andrew and Abby continued to love Levi through midnight screams, dirty diapers, and many messes. They continued to serve him day after day. They continued to provide for him. They still do today. The only thing they receive in return is the relationship.

Andrew and Abby's love for Levi will shape and mold his life. He is learning love from them.

Four years later, I spent a weekend with Andrew and Abby and their family. I was going through difficult circumstances, and at four years old, Levi could tell that something was wrong. As we were playing one evening, he asked me, "What do you feel?"

"I feel sad," I said.

"Jesus loves you. Jesus loves you and will make you feel better," Levi said. He was so confident.

He decided to cheer me up with a game of tag.

I know where he learned that Jesus loves, and I know where He developed the confidence that Jesus loves me. He learned it from the love of God and the Spirit of God working through His parents. That love had transformed him enough at four years old that he could comfort me with the truth. Love changes us.

God is the source of this love. He loves us instantly. He serves us and provides for us. We have so little to contribute. He loves us solely for the sake of the relationship.

CONVINCED OF GOD'S LOVE

Romans 8:31-32 – What then shall we say to these things? If God is for us, who can be against us? He who did not spare His own Son, but

delivered Him up for us all, how shall He not
with Him also freely give us all things?

God gave the greatest gift and sacrifice of all time—
Jesus Christ, His Son. Because God gave us Jesus, we
know He will give us all things. You can look at the
sacrifice of Jesus Christ and have confidence that whatever
you need, whoever you are, and whatever situation you are
in, God will provide because He has already given you all
spiritual things in Jesus. Ephesians 1:3 states that we have
already been blessed with every spiritual blessing in Christ.
Paul wrote that you can look at the cross, and you can
know that God loves you and that He is willing and able to
give you everything you need.

> **Romans 8:33 –** Who shall bring a charge against
> God's elect? It is God who justifies.

I was a sinner, but no one can accuse me for what
I've done in the past. I stand before God righteous and
without shame. I know my track record. I know my
history. I know I am righteous because it is God who has
justified me through the blood of Jesus.

You don't have to live in guilt and shame either.
You can't be stained or accused of anything if you put your
trust and faith in the God who forgives and transforms.
No one can lay a charge against you.

> **Romans 8:34-37 –** Who is He who condemns? It
> is Christ who died, and furthermore is also risen,
> who is even at the right hand of God, who also
> makes intercession for us. Who shall separate us
> from the love of Christ? Shall tribulation, or

> distress, or persecution, or famine, or
> nakedness, or peril, or sword? As it is written:
> "For Your sake we are killed all day long; we are
> accounted as sheep for the slaughter." Yet in all
> these things we are more than conquerors
> through Him who loved us.

God loves you. God, who is the Almighty, who created the heavens and the earth, who knows time from the beginning to the end, who set the world into motion, who parted the Red Sea, who sees every sin and every mistake and is altogether holy—looks down from heaven, and He says, "I love you."

Knowing this deeply provides unshakeable security. It doesn't matter what trouble you are in. God loves you. It doesn't matter what problem you have, the love of God is on your side.

God has given you His entire heart. He has held nothing back from you. He has given Jesus to you. God's commitment to you is total.

Paul wrote that in the midst of everything that we've been through, in everything that has been done to us, and in every attack of the enemy, we are more than conquerors. A conqueror is someone who has overcome and won the victory. Paul wrote that the word "conqueror" is not enough to describe what we are in Christ.

You are more than a conqueror. We may think that it's an act of faith to wake up in the morning and say, "I am a conqueror today." Paul wrote that that's not enough—you are more than a conqueror. He didn't have a word to describe how overcoming and how conquering you are because of God's love for you.

You are more than a conqueror through God who loves you. Because God loves you, you have more than overcome. God's love has covered you in the blood of the Lamb and given you a testimony of victory (Revelation 12:11). You will stand before Jesus, surrounded by His love and glory—alive forever in His victory.

You can be secure in the love of God that has won every victory, provided every sacrifice, done all the work, and has seated you in heavenly places with Christ Jesus. God's love never fails.

> **Romans 8:38-39 –** For I am persuaded that neither death nor life, nor angels nor principalities nor powers, nor things present nor things to come, nor height nor depth, nor any other created thing, shall be able to separate us from the love of God which is in Christ Jesus our Lord.

Paul was persuaded. He was completely convinced that nothing would separate us from God's great love. He was persuaded and wrote persuasively. God speaks through Paul to persuade you that nothing can separate you from His love. God says, "I have given you my heart, and nothing will make me take it back. I have given you my Son, and no sacrifice, no sin, no problem, no issue will ever undo the cross of Jesus Christ."

God loves you, and nothing can separate you from that love.

PAUL'S PRAYER FOR THE EPHESIANS

The Ephesian church was arguably the most mature

and healthy of the New Testament churches. Paul stayed there the longest during his third missionary journey and spent the most time raising up leaders and equipping the believers (Acts 19:9-10). Paul had very little correction for them in his epistle, and Ephesians contains some of the deepest revelation regarding our individual and corporate identity in Christ. Paul recorded his prayer for these believers:

> **Ephesians 3:14-21 –** For this reason I bow my knees to the Father of our Lord Jesus Christ, from whom the whole family in heaven and earth is named, that He would grant you, according to the riches of His glory, to be strengthened with might through His Spirit in the inner man, that Christ may dwell in your hearts through faith; that you, being rooted and grounded in love, may be able to comprehend with all the saints what is the width and length and depth and height—to know the love of Christ which passes knowledge; that you may be filled with all the fullness of God.
>
> Now to Him who is able to do exceedingly abundantly above all that we ask or think, according to the power that works in us, to Him be glory in the church by Christ Jesus to all generations, forever and ever. Amen.

Paul was on his knees praying that these mature believers would really know that God loved them.

Paul didn't record a prayer for their ministry. Paul didn't record a prayer for revival. He didn't pray that God would give them more understanding of the times and seasons. He didn't ask God to give them more Bible knowledge or miracles. He prayed that they would genuinely understand and know that God loved them.

He prayed that they would have their roots deep in the truth that God loved them. Paul wanted it to be more than just nice words or feelings to them but a deep, defining revelation. He wanted God's love to be their foundation for life.

God is so crazy about you, so "into" you, and so over-the-top about you that He sacrificed Himself for you while you were still a sinner (Romans 5:8). While you were still screwing it up, when you didn't believe the right things, when you were behaving the wrong way, and when you had no interest in Him—He died for you. He gave everything to you and held nothing back. That's who God is.

Paul prayed for the Ephesians that they would comprehend this love—that they would "get it." He wanted everyone to dive into the unending revelation of how wide, long, deep, and high the love of God is. He told them that it went beyond knowledge. It is impossible to reach the end of God's love. But He prayed that they would get a grip on the love of Christ.

He prayed that they would be filled with all the fullness of God. He wanted their lives to be saturated with God. God is love (1 John 4:8).

GOD IS LOVE

> **1 John 4:7-21 –** Beloved, let us love one
> another, for love is of God; and everyone who
> loves is born of God and knows God. He who

does not love does not know God, for God is
love. In this the love of God was manifested
toward us, that God has sent His only begotten
Son into the world, that we might live through
Him.

Jesus is how God's love showed up for you and me.
John wrote that God's love was manifested to us by the
arrival of Jesus into the world. Jesus—the revealed love of
God—lives forever, and we live through Him.

We can be so fickle. When bad things happen, we
wonder where God is. We wonder if God still loves us. A
bill comes at the wrong time. Our family forsakes us.
Things fall apart. Deep in our hearts we ask, "God, don't
you love me?"

John wrote that God has revealed His love once and
for all. He has proven it forever because He sent His one
and only Son, Jesus Christ.

Jesus was in eternity for all time—the Alpha and
the Omega, the Beginning and the End. He was sitting in
the glory of the angels. He was sitting in the worship of
heaven. He was the only one they found worthy to redeem
humanity. He was the spotless Lamb of God. Jesus chose
to leave all His glory. He put aside all of His possessions.
He put aside the praise and the worship. He was born into
the world as a baby. He went through human suffering. He
showed the love of God by healing the sick, cleansing the
leper, touching the untouchable, forgiving the sinners, and
setting captives free. He taught righteousness. He taught
love. And He did not condemn sinners; He empowered
them—He loosed them from their chains. Then He laid
down His life at the cross.

He let Roman soldiers put nails through His feet and hands. He let them pierce His side. And when the blood ran out, it paid the price for the redemption of every single human being.

But death couldn't hold Him. He couldn't be locked up. He took back the keys of hell, death, and the grave. He rose from the dead, and He will never die again. He lives forever to love us and spread His love throughout the earth.

That's what Jesus did for you. He did it because He loves you. He did it because he cares for you. He did it because you are worth it. He bought you with his blood. And you were worth the price.

God is thinking about you constantly (Psalm 139). In the Song of Solomon, the groom says, "You have ravished my heart with one look of your eyes" (4:9). One glance of your eyes makes God's heart leap. That's how Jesus feels about you.

> **1 John 4:10-11 –** In this is love, not that we loved God, but that He loved us and sent His Son to be the propitiation for our sins. Beloved, if God so loved us, we also ought to love one another.

It's not that we loved God, but that He loved us. God didn't say, "Because they love Me, I'll give them My Son," or, "Because they love Me, I'll love them." At the cross He said, "I love you even if you'll never love Me, and I'll give you My heart even if you trample on it. I'll hold nothing back from you. Even though you could walk away, it is worth the risk to seek and to save that which was lost."

He loves you and forgives you for free.

> **Roman 5:6-8 –** For when we were still without strength, in due time Christ died for the ungodly. For scarcely for a righteous man will one die; yet perhaps for a good man someone would even dare to die. But God demonstrates His own love toward us, in that while we were still sinners, Christ died for us.

I used to think that God loved right beliefs and right behavior. I thought that if I had right beliefs and right behavior, then God would love me. The truth is that when your beliefs were wrong and your behavior was screwed up, God still loved you. He still loved you because He is love, and His love is free. There is nothing that you can do to earn it, and there's nothing that you can do to lose it. His love is eternal. It endures. It never fails.

God's love can be mixed with pain or grief. God's love can exist alongside anger. But God's love never goes away. It endures. God's loving self-sacrifice for us has existed before the beginning of the world (Revelation 13:8).

> **1 John 4:12 –** No one has seen God at any time. If we love one another, God abides in us, and His love has been perfected in us.

We were created to show God to the world. When Adam looked at Eve, he could see perfect love. When she looked at him, she could see perfect love. We were designed to represent God, and we lost that in the fall. But we were still designed to look at one another and to see what God looks like.

The world is looking at humanity, and they are asking, "Where is God? If God is so good why does humanity look like this?" They are still looking for God in people. The world no longer displays the image of God. If we love one another and display the love that we've been shown, we will reveal God to the world.

ABIDING IN LOVE

Romans 5:5 – Now hope does not disappoint, because the love of God has been poured out in our hearts by the Holy Spirit who was given to us.

The Spirit of God pours His love into our hearts. The Holy Spirit can make you like Jesus. He reveals love, and He deposits love within us as we receive from Him.

In the pattern of Zechariah 4:6, "Not by might or by power but by the Spirit" you can be transformed into the love that you were always created to be.

1 John 4:13-16 – By this we know that we abide in Him, and He in us, because He has given us of His Spirit. And we have seen and testify that the Father has sent the Son as Savior of the world. Whoever confesses that Jesus is the Son of God, God abides in him, and he in God. And we have known and believed the love that God has for us. God is love, and he who abides in love abides in God, and God in him.

Being a believer means knowing and believing that God loves you. Believing that Jesus died on the cross and rose from the dead includes the knowledge that God loves us so much that He gave Jesus as the sacrifice for our sins. Truly knowing God's love for us defines us as the people of God.

Part of our Christian walk and our transformation is living in that love. John equated abiding in God's love with abiding in God and God abiding in us. We live in God's love. God's love lives in us.

> **Jude 1:20-21 –** But you, beloved, building yourselves up on your most holy faith, praying in the Holy Spirit, keep yourselves in the love of God, looking for the mercy of our Lord Jesus Christ unto eternal life.

My parents told me often that they loved me. As a child, I felt secure in their love; but as I got older and life became harder, I lost that security. I no longer grasped that my parents loved me on a deep level. I doubted their love. I became angry with them. I rebelled. I became blind to their sacrifices for me. I couldn't see their constant gifts and service. I took them for granted and failed to acknowledge their love. Their love for me didn't change, but I couldn't see their love in the midst of the pain of life.

We can't change God's love for us, but we can change how we receive that love. We can walk away from God's love. We can doubt God's love. We can deny God's love. Or we can freely receive and live in the love of the Father. We can keep ourselves in the love of God.

Abiding, remaining, and keeping ourselves in the love of God means a daily walk in the acknowledgement of God's love for us. We believe it. We receive and accept it. We trust it regardless of trials or circumstances. We don't let circumstances overwhelm our faith in the everlasting love of God. We let God's love direct our thoughts and actions. Our feelings follow and respond to this love we see.

We saturate ourselves with the gospel—the good news of God's love demonstrated and proven forever on the cross. We look beyond the pain and trials of this world, and we see love. We look at Jesus and say without doubt, "God loves me. God loves me forever." The process of prophetic transformation is walking day by day in response to the Spirit's revelation of God's transforming love.

Epilogue
Don't Look Back

Luke 17:31-36 – Jesus said, "In that day, he who is on the housetop, and his goods are in the house, let him not come down to take them away. And likewise the one who is in the field, let him not turn back. Remember Lot's wife. Whoever seeks to save his life will lose it, and whoever loses his life will preserve it. I tell you, in that night there will be two men in one bed: the one will be taken and the other will be left. Two women will be grinding together: the one will be taken and the other left. Two men will be in the field: the one will be taken and the other left."

Genesis 12:1 – God spoke to Abraham and said, "Get out of your country, from your family and from your father's house, to a land that I will show you."

By faith, Abraham made the decision to obey the voice of God; and by that faith-decision, he was declared righteous for all eternity. Abraham's nephew Lot agreed to go with him. Because Lot left the worship of idols and journeyed with Abraham, he was also declared righteous (2 Peter 2:7).

Abraham and Lot both fell into gross immorality. We tend to gloss over these sins because the stories seem so far removed from us and because they are often varnished with a religious sheen.

Abraham and Lot held slaves. Abraham forced Sarah's female servant into a sexual relationship. They lied. Lot committed incest. Yet at the end of their lives, the Bible calls them righteous because they left everything to follow the voice of God. We are not saved by our works. We are saved by grace through faith.

Abraham and Lot left their old lives and idols behind to go on the journey that God commanded. They decided that they would not turn back. They would not stop worshipping God. They would not stop following him.

Abraham and Lot came to a place where they chose different paths. They came to a land where they were going to settle, and conflict forced them to part ways. Abraham, in his love and trust toward God, offered Lot the pick of the land. Lot, in his selfishness, chose what he believed was the best location.

> **Genesis 13:10-13 –** And Lot lifted his eyes and saw all the plain of Jordan, that it was well watered everywhere (before the Lord destroyed Sodom and Gomorrah) like the garden of the

> Lord, like the land of Egypt as you go toward
> Zoar. Then Lot chose for himself all the plain of
> Jordan, and Lot journeyed east. And they
> separated from each other. Abram dwelt in the
> land of Canaan, and Lot dwelt in the cities of the
> plain and pitched his tent even as far as Sodom.
> But the men of Sodom were exceedingly wicked
> and sinful against the Lord.

In the midst of all of Abraham's mistakes and failures, God spoke to Abraham, and Abraham listened. Abraham became a friend of God (James 2:23). Abraham continued to repent of his ways, and God continued to forgive him. Abraham continued to change. He continued to worship God. God confided in him.

God told Abraham, "I am going to destroy Sodom and Gomorrah" (Genesis 18:20-21, 19:13). Abraham interceded, and God promised not to destroy the city if ten righteous people could be found. God sent two angels to see the wickedness of the city and to rescue Lot. Lot had made his home in the midst of wickedness, but because of Abraham's faith, God sent angels to pull Lot out of the evil where he lived.

> **Genesis 19:1-5 –** Now the two angels came to
> Sodom in the evening, and Lot was sitting in the
> gate of Sodom. When Lot saw them, he rose to
> meet them, and he bowed himself with his face
> toward the ground. And he said, "Here now, my
> lords, please turn in to your servant's house and
> spend the night, and wash your feet; then you
> may rise early and go on your way."
>
> And they said, "No, but we will spend the

> night in the open square."
>
> But he insisted strongly; so they turned in to him and entered his house. Then he made them a feast and baked unleavened bread, and they ate.
>
> Now before they lay down, the men of the city, the men of Sodom, both old and young, all the people from every quarter, surrounded the house. And they called to Lot and said to him, "Where are the men who came to you tonight? Bring them out to us that we may know them carnally."

The city of Sodom was so evil that this was a common practice. Sodom became famous for this incident. The name of the city became the word for a certain sexual act. Yet despite the reputation and the definition that Sodom now has, their sin was more grievous than simple homosexuality. Essentially, the men of the city are saying, "Bring these strangers out so that we can gang rape them." These men were so depraved and their culture so perverted that instead of offering strangers hospitality, they were consumed with lust to publically sexually abuse and rape other men. This is the unified behavior of the men of the city. This had happened before. This was their practice and their culture. Lot had decided to live and stay in this city and this culture.

> **Genesis 19:6-7 –** So Lot went out to them through the doorway, shut the door behind him, and said, "Please, my brethren, do not do so wickedly! See now, I have two daughters who have not known a man; please, let me bring

> them out to you, and you may do to them as
> you wish; only do nothing to these men, since
> this is the reason they have come under the
> shadow of my roof."

Lot's behavior is even more shocking. He is so accustomed to this behavior and so callous toward others that he offered his virgin daughters to the crowd. He hoped they would be satisfied by abusing his own daughters. Lot was so blinded and so perverted by living in this society that he believed this action was an appropriate response to the crowd. He believed that he was acting better than they were. His actions were unthinkable.

This is where sin takes us. It blinds. It deceives. It wears us down until righteousness is forgotten completely, and we consider heinous immorality moral because it's slightly above the morality of our culture.

We can read this story and think that it is far removed from our culture. It is not. Any device with a web browser could access this kind of entertainment material within five seconds. Our culture has laws that contain this evil as best it can. It sets up regulations that permit it to be acted out and viewed. The heart of our culture is no better than Sodom.

> **Genesis 19:9 –** And they said, "Stand back!"
> Then they said, "This one came in to stay here,
> and he keeps acting as a judge; now we will deal
> worse with you than with them." So they
> pressed hard against the man Lot, and came
> near to break down the door.

The crowd's response is much like our culture's

today. They shouted, "You're judging me." They were about to gang rape two men; and when someone said, "This is evil. Don't do it," they responded, "How dare you judge us?"

Sin destroys people. Sin was not what humanity was made for. Sin warps the mind until rationality, conscience, and morality is lost.

I remember sharing the Gospel on the street and coming across a man, who was addicted to alcohol. I prayed for him; and when I prayed, "Lord, deliver this man from the addiction to alcohol," he interrupted me and shouted, "No, God! I want to keep drinking alcohol!"

I thought, *Are you crazy? You're out here in the middle of the street in a dirty shirt, drunk at twelve in the afternoon. And you are praying that God will let you keep your sin? What is wrong with you?* This is what sin does to people. It harms their mind. It deceives.

People refuse to change. They are bound in their hearts and their minds. They begin to think that this is what God made them for. They don't see that Jesus died for them. They don't see that they're worth the blood of Jesus. They don't understand that God loves them. They don't see that God wants to give them a miracle—to change them into something wonderful. They don't see that God has a vision of them as men and women of honor with the Word of God and the Spirit of God within them. They can't see that God made them with a value and purpose—to be valuable to this world. They can't see their unique value—that God made them to demonstrate Jesus in a way that only they can for all of eternity. They can't understand that God designed them from the beginning of the world because He loved them and had them in His heart.

They hold onto their sin. They don't desire to change.

The man who wanted to keep his alcohol said, "You're judging me."

I said, "The Bible says, 'no drunkard will enter the kingdom.'"

He was angry with me. Like the men of Sodom, this man was living in a place that was about to be destroyed. He needed to escape immediately.

Lot's words fell to the ground. The townsmen knew that Lot lived among them. They knew that he took part in their culture. They knew that he sat by passively when these things happened before. He had no moral ground to stand on.

> **Genesis 19:9-11 –** And they said, "Stand back!" Then they said, "This one came in to stay here, and he keeps acting as a judge; now we will deal worse with you than with them." So they pressed hard against the man Lot, and came near to break down the door. But the men reached out their hands and pulled Lot into the house with them, and shut the door. And they struck the men who were at the doorway of the house with blindness, both small and great, so that they became weary trying to find the door.

The angels performed a miracle in front of the whole crowd and blinded all of the men at the door. What is even more chilling is that even after being miraculously struck blind by angels these men still try to find the door. They are supernaturally blinded by an angel and instead of thinking, Wait! There must be something wrong, they groped at the door to try to finish what they started. These men's evil desires and lusts had so consumed their minds and hearts that even though God intervened with a miracle they had no capacity to stop.

Sin has no boundaries. If you let it, it will completely take over your life.

In the same way that sin and hatred and lust can take over people, love and the Holy Spirit can take over people. These men were compelled by lust. Paul said, "I am compelled by love" (2 Corinthians 5:14).

When sin compels people, the results are horrifying. When love compels people, they change the world.

> **Genesis 19:12-13 –** Then the [angels] said to Lot, "Have you anyone else here? Son-in-law, your sons, your daughters, and whomever you have in the city—take them out of this place! For we will destroy this place, because the outcry against them has grown great before the face of the Lord, and the Lord has sent us to destroy it."

The angels tell Lot, "This place of sin, this place of depravity where you are living, is going to be destroyed. You must get out, and anyone else you can convince to come with you." The fire of destruction was coming. Today, God holds back the fire of judgment, not willing that anyone perish but that all might come to repentance (2 Peter 3:9).

Repentance is the way to escape destruction. Repentance is the way to escape death. This message is true today. God's fire of judgment is coming on sin. A day is coming when fire will destroy all evil, all sin, and all who live in it. On that day those who are declared innocent will be free because of the blood of the Lamb, Jesus Christ.

We have the same charge that Lot had. Our families, the people who are "family" to us, must be pulled out of sin. Go and compel them to leave darkness and enter into light.

> **Genesis 19:14 –** So Lot went out and spoke to his sons-in-law, who had married his daughters, and said, "Get up, get out of this place; for the Lord will destroy this city!" But to his sons-in-law he seemed to be joking.

Many respond the same way today. The gospel is not real to them. The consequences of sin are not real to them. They think, This sin will not really destroy my life. It is not serious to them. Eternity is not real to them.

> **Genesis 19:15-16 –** When the morning dawned, the angels urged Lot to hurry, saying, "Arise, take your wife and your two daughters who are here, lest you be consumed in the punishment of the city." And while he lingered, the men took hold of his hand, his wife's hand, and the hands of his two daughters, the Lord being merciful to him, and they brought him out and set him outside the city.

When the angels told Lot that the entire area would be destroyed, he hesitated. He lingered. He didn't want to leave yet. He wanted a few more hours, a few more minutes. He thought he had more time. He didn't.

If you are living in sin, you don't have more time.

Jesus is coming soon. Time is running out. Today is the day of salvation. Tomorrow is not guaranteed.

There is not much time to become all that Jesus paid for you to be. Jesus paid for you to be like Him. He paid for you to carry the presence of God. He paid for you to carry the love of God. He has a plan and a calling for you. We don't have much time. We have to change now.

Lot lingered. He didn't want to change yet. He didn't want to leave the place of sin yet.

The angels won't take no for an answer. They grabbed Lot and his wife's hands and the hands of his daughters and, in the Lord's mercy, dragged them out of the city by force. I thank God for the times that He has dragged me. But I know that I can't count on that.

I want to have the zeal and the passion to grab others and drag them—to snatch them out of the fire (Jude 1:23) and compel them to come in (Luke 14:23).

> **Genesis 19:17 –** So it came to pass, when they had brought them outside, that he said, "Escape for your life! Do not look behind you nor stay anywhere in the plain. Escape to the mountains, lest you be destroyed."

God had dragged them out of the thick of it. But they still had a choice. They still had to run.

God saved me. He pulled me out of the thick of sin and darkness. He pointed the direction and told me to run.

Run for safety. Run for the prize. Run for victory. Run for the high calling of God in Christ Jesus. Go fast. Go hard. Don't stop. Don't look back.

Genesis 19:19-20 – Then Lot said to them,
"Please, no, my lords! Indeed now, your servant
has found favor in your sight, and you have
increased your mercy, which you have shown
me by saving my life; but I cannot escape to the
mountains, lest some evil overtake me and I die.
See now, this city is near enough to flee to, and
it is a little one; please let me escape there (is it
not a little one?) and my soul shall live."

Lot begged for a compromise. God promised Lot a
place in the mountains. Lot wanted a place in the plains.
He didn't trust God's plan. He wanted one edge of sinful
civilization. He wanted God to spare some small space in
the sinful land for him to go. God allowed Lot to do it.
God will allow you to live a life of compromise. Later, Lot
left that city, too. We can compromise for a time, but in
the end the area of compromise will also be destroyed. It
may not be the depths of sin, but it is not God's will for
your life. We often want to settle for less than God's plan
for us. In God's patience and mercy, He waits for us to
move on.

Genesis 19:21-26 – And [the angel] said to [Lot],
"See, I have favored you concerning this thing
also, in that I will not overthrow this city for
which you have spoken. Hurry, escape there. For
I cannot do anything until you arrive there."
Therefore the name of the city was called Zoar.
The sun had risen upon the earth when Lot
entered Zoar. Then the Lord rained brimstone
and fire on Sodom and Gomorrah, from the Lord
out of the heavens. So He overthrew those

> cities, all the plain, all the inhabitants of the
> cities, and what grew on the ground.
> But his wife looked back behind him, and she
> became a pillar of salt.

In the midst of dramatic rescue, Lot's wife looked back at the land of depravity. She gazed longingly at it, thinking, That's my home. That's the place I love. That's the place where I was comfortable. That's the place where people liked me. That's the place where I had status. That's the place where I had pleasure. That's the place where I had possessions. She was destroyed.

Jesus said, "Remember Lot's wife. Whoever seeks to save his life will lose it, and whoever loses his life will preserve it" (Luke 17:32-33).

We were not made to have a selfish right over our own life. When Adam lived in the garden, he had no claim over his own life. His life totally belonged to God. When he ate of the Tree of the Knowledge of Good and Evil, he gained the right to make the decisions for himself. He gained the right to cling to his own life.

But you were never made to run your own life. You were never made to make selfish decisions. You were never made to decide for yourself.

Eternal life is found in giving our lives and rights to the One who created us. The eternal quality of life is found in giving our lives to the One who purchased us with His own blood. When we lose our lives to Jesus, He floods our lives with an eternal, overcoming Life.

God has a way for us and a place for us in His love. We are meant to move forward into this love. It is a place of self-sacrifice. It is worth everything to get there. It is worth everything to change. Pain and sorrow are worth it if we can be changed. Inconvenience and loss are worth it if we can be free and change. God has a better plan for all of us.

You have a new identity in Christ. You are seated at the right hand of God, hidden in Jesus. You are blessed, made righteous, and made whole. That is who you are in the Spirit.

Will you choose that love that God has placed inside you? Will you choose that love that has been shed abroad in your heart by the Holy Spirit? Will you choose love over the desires of the flesh and the desires of the world? Will you change?

We must have our eyes fixed on Jesus and move closer and closer to His glory and perfect image. We look into the mirror of the Word, and we see that God has made us righteous. God has made us whole. God has made us holy. God has made us powerful. God has made us loving. We walk away transformed into the person we have seen in Christ.

Works Cited

Ton, Josef. *Suffering, Martyrdom, and Rewards in Heaven.* The Romanian Missionary Society, 2000.

Rich, Nathaniel. "Can a Jellyfish Unlock the Secret of Immortality?" The New York Times Magazine. The New York Times. 28 Nov. 2012. 13 Dec. 2016.

From the Author

I want to thank you so much for reading Prophetic Transformation and spending time with my story. I would love to connect with. You can contact me at JonathanAndTatianaAmmon@gmail.com and at sentlives.com. I would love to know what you think about the book. You are the reason I am writing, and you are important to me. I also would really appreciate it if you left a review on Amazon or Goodreads.

About the Author

Jonathan Ammon lives and serves Jesus among the unreached. He participates in movements of churches by bringing the Good News of Christ's kingdom and raising up laborers and leaders. Jonathan's writing focuses on holiness and faithfully hearing and proclaiming God's message.

You can learn more about Jonathan's ministry at
www.SentLives.com

ADDITIONAL RESOURCES:

More books by this author:

➢ *Voice of God 40-Day Hearing God Activation Manual* by Jonathan Ammon, Art Thomas, and James Loruss

➢ *Paid in Full 40-Day Healing Ministry Activation Manual* by Jonathan Ammon, Art Thomas, and James Loruss

For learning more about hearing God's voice and prophetic ministry:

➢ *Voice of God* (DVD movie)

➢ *Voice of God* 8-Week Small Group DVD and Curriculum (DVD and PDF download)

➢ *The Word of Knowledge in Action* (Book)

All materials are available at www.SupernaturalTruth.com

There are also plenty of **free videos, articles, and audio sermons** under the "Free Media" tab at www.SupernaturalTruth.com.

Please consider sharing this book with a friend and writing a review on Amazon.com.

Additional copies available at
www.SupernaturalTruth.com